JFK Assassination Eyewitness:
Rush

My thanks to my daughters Julie and Christy Kay, my son-in-law David and my friend Lyn for their invaluable help and David Perry for sharing his research.

JFK
ASSASSINATION EYEWITNESS:
RUSH
TO CONSPIRACY
THE REAL FACTS OF LEE BOWERS' DEATH

ANITA DICKASON

ARCHWAY
PUBLISHING

Archway Publishing books may be ordered through booksellers or by contacting:

Archway Publishing
1663 Liberty Drive
Bloomington, IN 47403
www.archwaypublishing.com
1-(888)-242-5904

Because of the dynamic nature of the Internet, any web addresses or links contained in this book may have changed since publication and may no longer be valid. The views expressed in this work are solely those of the author and do not necessarily reflect the views of the publisher, and the publisher hereby disclaims any responsibility for them.

Any people depicted in stock imagery provided by Thinkstock are models, and such images are being used for illustrative purposes only.
Certain stock imagery © Thinkstock.

ISBN: 978-1-4808-0335-0 (sc)
ISBN: 978-1-4808-0336-7 (e)

Library of Congress Control Number: 2013918161

Printed in the United States of America

Archway Publishing rev. date: 10/29/2013

TABLE OF CONTENTS

CHAPTER 1

Introduction

On November 22, 1963, Lee Bowers, Jr. became a key witness to the assassination of President John F. Kennedy. Less than three years later, he was killed in a one-car accident southwest of Midlothian, Texas under mysterious circumstances. His name was added to a list of individuals associated with the investigation of the Kennedy assassination who had allegedly died under suspicious circumstances.

A few months before his death, Mark Lane interviewed Bowers for his book: *Rush to Judgment*.[1] Bowers' statements in the Mark Lane interview, plus the conflicting information regarding the accident, added fuel to the conspiracy theories. Was Bowers killed because of what he saw on the day President Kennedy was shot and killed? Was there something unusual regarding the car accident? Was his car run off the road by another vehicle? Was he able to talk to ambulance personnel and did he tell them he had been drugged at a coffee shop prior to the accident? Was he in a strange state of shock? This is a forty-seven year-old mystery that involved a motor vehicle accident.

As a retired advanced accident investigator, I conduct cold case accident investigations. I had not heard of the Lee Bowers' case until I was contacted by Indigo Films regarding a new series: America Declassified. An episode on JFK was going to include the Bowers' accident and I was asked to participate in the episode. I had only a short time for research prior to the taping of the show. The details I was able to identify left me with more questions than answers. What were the real facts behind the Bowers' accident? Finding the answers meant attempting the reconstruction of a 1966 accident. A full cold case accident investigation would certainly push the limits on identifying any pertinent details of the accident. The research became every bit as difficult as I anticipated and continued for several months after the completion of the segment for America Declassified. The Bowers' accident developed into the type of case I categorize as an "investigative hook." It's a case that grabs you and does not let go.

I am uniquely qualified to conduct cold case accident investigations. I have a total of twenty-seven years law enforcement experience with twenty-two years with the Dallas Police Department. My field experience, combined with my involvement with the department's accident report system, provides an in-depth level of knowledge and experience of accident investigation, the Texas accident report system and Texas Traffic Law.

I was assigned to the department's Traffic Division. Traffic officers receive specialized accident investigation training and are responsible for the investigation of all traffic fatality accidents and accidents involving city vehicles. The Traffic Division is also responsible for the administration of the department's accident report system. Not all accidents that occur in Dallas are investigated by Traffic officers. The city of Dallas is geographically divided into seven patrol divisions. The majority of accidents, not resulting in a fatality or involving a city vehicle, are investigated by patrol officers. The reason is due to the number of accidents per year and the limited resources of the Traffic Division. When I transferred to the Traffic Division in 2000, the department was investigating approximately 30,000 accidents per year. Part of my responsibilities dealt with evaluating an officer's investigation of an accident and the accident report and returning reports requiring correction to the officer. For a period of time, all accident reports were sent to me for review and approval. Over a ten year period I have analyzed thousands of accident investigations and subsequent reports. I developed the procedures for an internal review program for the patrol divisions. I developed a number of the department's training programs for accident investigation and reporting procedures and have trained over 5000 officers. I was the department's liaison to the Texas Department of Transportation Crash Report Division and as such assisted in the development of the current accident report format and the State of Texas Instructions to Police for Reporting Crashes manual. I have testified before the Texas Department of Transportation Vehicle and Crash Report Divisions regarding accident report investigation, accident statistical analysis and the operation of motorized devices on Texas roadways.

There was one other area of responsibility that proved to be particularly valuable in the research and analysis of the Bowers' accident. I received a copy of every autopsy report involving a traffic fatality from the Dallas County Medical Examiner's office. Traffic fatalities include not only the drivers and passengers in the vehicle but also pedestrians who were killed by a motor vehicle. This was approximately 125-150 reports per year and spanned a ten year period. It was necessary to review each report for information regarding the blood test results. The accident report had to be amended to add the test results or indicate when a test was not conducted. I gained considerable knowledge from the medical description of the victim's injuries in relationship to the type of collision, as well as other contributing factors to the injuries (position in the vehicle, seat belt use, ejection, etc.)

A cold case accident investigation is an analysis of the accuracy of a law enforcement officer's investigation of a motor vehicle accident and the subsequent accident report. Typical cases will range from weeks to over a year old and as such require a different level of research and analysis. The process is significantly different from the standard types of accident reconstruction. This is due to the interval between the date of the accident and the reconstruction investigation. Standard types of reconstruction service involve an investigation that occurs as close to the date of the accident as possible. Immediate access to the accident scene is necessary, allowing for measurements of skid marks to determine speed, direction of travel, impact points and identify other physical evidence that contributed to the accident. There is usually a short window of time for this type of investigation, as roadway evidence can become contaminated by vehicular traffic and weather conditions. It is expensive and is typically utilized in high profile or high dollar law suits. A cold case accident investigation is conducted weeks to months after the accident has occurred and is based on the law enforcement officer's investigation and report.

Understanding the methods involved in a cold case accident investigation requires an explanation of the existing problems in accident investigations and reports. It is a known fact, accidents investigated by law enforcement officers will not always result in an accurate investigation or subsequent report. This, in part, is due to inadequate or lack of training, poor investigative procedures, attitude and even incompetence. Furthermore, many law enforcement agencies do not have an internal review process to ensure the accuracy of the investigation or report. The reasons are many and vary from department to department: a perception the report is only for the insurance company, departmental structure and prioritization of resources are just a few examples. Unfortunately, the bottom line for many investigations is the wrong person is blamed for the accident. It is not unusual for the person, wrongly charged with the accident, to receive a corresponding citation for traffic violations, which were invalid or did not even exist.

The consequences of an accident are far-reaching and do not end with the investigation or the completion of an accident report. Errors affect insurance settlements, insurance rates, civil lawsuits, driving history and more importantly, they affect the individuals in the vehicles and family members.

A cold case accident investigation is all about the people involved with the accident: what did they do and what should they have done. What was the end result of their actions and were there any other conditions such as roadway, environmental, legal, medical or vehicular, which contributed to the final result? Does the physical evidence, such as the damage to the vehicles, support the statements of the driver and any witnesses? The analysis of these issues determines whether the accident could have physically occurred as reported by the investigating officer.

I analyze the information in the accident report, vehicle damage, layout of the accident site, environmental and roadway conditions, driver/witness statements and the legal applicability of the report information. It is a comprehensive evaluation to identify inconsistencies or errors affecting the assignment of driver liability by the investigating officer.

The methodology I developed for cold case accident investigations would need to be modified for the investigation of the Bowers' accident. The typical elements in a cold case accident investigation were missing. I did not have an accident report. I did not have a vehicle to assess damage, direction of force or impact points. Initially, even the accident site was a major issue as I discovered the site selected by the film company was on a relatively new section of highway that did not exist in 1966. My research would have to extend beyond the normal scope of an investigation. It would need to include an assessment of existing documents and publications for information on the accident. The necessity to factor in the 1966 Texas Traffic Laws would further compound the difficulties of the research.

Considering the controversy that has swirled around the Bowers' accident, I could not ignore the events of Bowers' life that led to the controversy. Researching the past life of an accident victim is not typically part of the analysis of a cold case accident investigation. Investigating a 1966 accident with a lot of missing information is also not the typical case. I soon realized, however, Bowers' background and the events leading to his death were intertwined. It was not possible to evaluate the accident without considering the totality of the life of Bowers, the role he played in the investigation of the Kennedy assassination, as well as the events surrounding the accident and his death. To state these were extreme difficulties would be an understatement at best.

JFK ASSASSINATION EYEWITNESS: Rush to Conspiracy is a step by step progression of the research and the analysis of the results with elements of Texas history thrown in along the way. The findings uncovered an unexpected twist in the aftermath of events of Lee Bowers' death on an August morning in 1966.

CHAPTER 2

The History

Lee Bowers, Jr. was born in 1925 in Dallas, Texas and continued to live in the Dallas area for most of his life. He graduated from Woodrow Wilson High School. He served in the U.S. Navy, during WWII, from the age of seventeen to twenty-one. After the war, Bowers attended Hardin-Simmons University and Southern Methodist University where he majored in religion. He worked for the Union Terminal Company for a number of years. He was the tower man assigned to the north tower and operated the switches and signals that controlled the movement of trains on the west side of downtown Dallas. In addition to his position with the railroad, he worked on the side as a self-employed builder in the Dallas real estate development market. By 1964, he had left the railroad and was working as a business manager for a local hospital and convalescent home. At the time of his death in 1966, he was Vice-President of Lochwood Meadows, Inc.

Bowers' life was probably not unusual. He served his country in WWII, as did many of his counterparts. He returned to civilian life to continue his education, marry and raise a family. Each day he went about his business of earning a living and supporting his family.

November 22, 1963 should have been a day just like any other workday for Bowers. He would have arrived at work, clocked in and began his shift. He had no idea that by the end of his shift he would play an integral role in one of the most traumatic events in American history. His life and ultimately his death would be forever linked to that fatal day in Dallas, Texas; Bowers was to become one of the key witnesses to the assassination of President John F. Kennedy.

Most Americans who are old enough to remember the day President Kennedy was assassinated can remember exactly where they were when they heard the horrific news. I was a freshman in college and had come home during the lunch break. As I walked into my home, my grandfather was watching the television, as the events in Dallas were being reported. I remember being absolutely stunned when I heard Walter Cronkite announce President Kennedy had been shot and killed. When I returned to the college everyone was being directed to assemble in the auditorium. What struck me, as I sat in that auditorium and what I still remember, was the absolute quiet in the room. Several hundred college students filled the room and none of them were talking. You could have heard the proverbial pin drop. It was as if everyone was in a state of shock.

Bowers had a front seat, up close and center stage, to the events as they unfolded. On November 22, 1963, he was working in a two story, fourteen-foot high railroad tower overlooking the parking lot just north of the grassy knoll and west of the Texas School Book Depository. Photo #1 is an aerial view of Dealey Plaza, the Texas School Book Depository and the adjacent parking lot.[2] The tower (indicated by the arrow) where Bowers was working is located at the north end of the parking lot. From Bowers' position in the tower, he had an unobstructed view of the area around the grassy knoll and behind the wooden fence. His testimony would ultimately lead to allegations his death was a result of what he saw on that fateful day.

#1

CHAPTER 3

The Witness

Bowers provided three documented accounts of what he observed on the day President John F. Kennedy was assassinated. The first was the Dallas Affidavit (Appendix 1), provided to local law enforcement on the day of the assassination, November 22, 1963.[3] The second was his testimony to the Warren Commission in 1964 (Appendix 2)[4] and the third was the 1966 Mark Lane interview[5].

Bowers' position in the railroad tower was an excellent location to observe the movement of pedestrians and cars in the area. It is not difficult to imagine, from his perch in the tower, he was a people and car watcher. In the Warren Commission testimony he indicated he had worked there for a number of years and was familiar with the movement of individuals in the area. Bowers was probably very alert to any suspicious activity.

From an investigator's perspective, I found Bowers' testimony extremely intriguing. He provided specific and detailed descriptions of vehicles, drivers, and pedestrians he observed in the area surrounding the Texas School Book Depository and the grassy knoll. What struck me was his attention to detail; this was very evident in all three interviews. This is not always the case when dealing with witness interviews or statements.

The Dallas Affidavit is a short and concise description of three vehicles he observed enter the parking lot in front of the tower where he was located. The first vehicle was a dirty 1959 Oldsmobile station wagon which came down the street in front of his location. This street dead ends into the railroad yard. The car had out of state license plates. Even though Bowers could not identify the state, he did describe the plate as having a white background and black numbers, with no letters. He also described the Goldwater for "64" sticker located in the rear window of the vehicle. According to Bowers the car, driven by a middle aged white man with partly grey hair, drove around slowly and then left the area. This occurred at about 11:55 a.m. At about 12:15 p.m. a second vehicle, a 1957 black 2-door Ford with Texas plates, drove into the area. The driver appeared to have a mike or telephone. The vehicle left about 12:20 p.m. A few minutes later the third vehicle entered the area. Bowers described the vehicle as a 1961 white 4-door Impala Chevrolet, though he did add he was not sure it was a 4-door. He stated the vehicle was dirty up to the windows and also had a Goldwater for "64" sticker. The vehicle was driven by a white male about 25-35 years old with long blond hair. Bowers stated this vehicle stayed in the area longer than the other two vehicles. The car had the same type of license plate as the first vehicle. The vehicle left the area at about 12:25 p.m. Bowers said that 8-10 minutes later he heard the three shots.

In the Warren Commission testimony, Bowers stated the area had been covered by the police for about two hours. Bowers also said the morning traffic had been cut off by the police at about 10:00 a.m. so that anyone moving around could actually be observed. I was on the Dallas Swat Team for several years. I worked numerous security details including several for presidential visits. Once an area had been cordoned off, pedestrians and vehicles were not allowed to enter without special clearance. The fact these vehicles were in the area after it had been closed by the police was extremely interesting. This was further enhanced by the description of the vehicles and the drivers. Bowers also provided additional details on the movement of the three vehicles. He indicated they appeared to be searching for a way out of the railroad yard but without success. The extension of Elm St was the only way in and out of the railroad yard.

The Warren Commission testimony included a number of other interesting details. Bowers stated he heard three shots. There was one, then a slight pause and another two very close together. Bowers was asked if he could form an opinion regarding the source or direction of the sound. Bowers stated the sounds came either from up against the School Depository building or near the mouth of the triple underpass. When specifically asked if he could tell which, he said no, he could not. Bowers indicated he saw two men standing on what would be the grassy knoll and, once again, was able to provide a detailed description of the two individuals. He identified several individuals standing on top of the triple underpass to include police officers, railroad employees and even two welders and their assistant. In the aftermath of the shooting, he described the actions of a motorcycle officer and other individuals who were moving into the area, including the two individuals he had previously identified as standing on the grassy knoll.

There is an interesting difference between the Dallas Affidavit and the Warren Commission testimony. The Dallas Affidavit only included the movement of the three vehicles and descriptions of the drivers. There was no information regarding any individuals or associated activity at the grassy knoll. It is a reflection of the change of direction the investigation of the assassination of President Kennedy had taken regarding the significance of the grassy knoll.

After the Warren Commission testimony there is no further documented activity of any interviews until the 1966 Mark Lane interview of Bowers. Mark Lane's book, *Rush to Judgment*, was released in August, 1966 and dealt with the conclusions of the Warren Commission. It gained best seller status. In 1967, a documentary film, *Rush to Judgment*, was produced based on Mark Lane's book. The documentary included Lane's taped interview of Bowers.

Bowers indicated, in the Lane interview, not everything he had seen on the day of the Kennedy assignation had been discussed in the testimony provided to the Warren Commission. This dealt with something that caught his attention in the area of the grassy knoll. Bowers indicated there was a flash of light, a puff of smoke or something he could not identify but was unusual.

A few months after the interview with Mark Lane, Bowers was dead. The conspiracy theories started to build.

CHAPTER 4

The Conspiracy Theories

On Tuesday, August 9, 1966, Bowers was killed as a result of injuries sustained in a one-car accident. Bowers was traveling alone in a 1965 Pontiac Catalina convertible and hit a bridge located on Highway 67, two miles southwest of Midlothian, Texas. He was transported to the Waxahachie hospital by ambulance and then transferred to Methodist hospital in Dallas. Judge W.E. Richburg, Justice of the Peace, Precinct 7, Dallas County pronounced death at 12:50 p.m.

After Bowers' death, reports began to surface he had received death threats as a result of the Warren Commission testimony and his statements in the Mark Lane interview. There were claims his death was not accidental and his death was due to what he saw the day President Kennedy was shot and killed.

The significance of these claims gained additional prominence when Bowers' name was added to a list of individuals who had died and had been associated with the Kennedy assassination. In 1978, the House Select Committee on Assassinations initiated an investigation on the circumstances of the death of twenty-one persons identified by various authors as connected to the Kennedy assassination. Bowers was #4 on the Library of Congress Congressional Research Service report titled *"Analysis of Reports and Data Bearing on Circumstances of Death of Twenty-one Individuals Connected with the Assassination of President John F. Kennedy."*[6] Two authors were cited in the report, Penn Jones, Jr. *Forgive My Grief, II (1967)*[7] and Richard Lewis, *The Scavengers and Critics of the Warren Report (1967).*[8]

Penn Jones, Jr. owned the Midlothian Mirror newspaper in Midlothian, TX and was also the editor. He was an outspoken critic of the Warren Commission and believed the government was behind the assassination of President Kennedy. Jones gained national recognition for his opinions. He wrote four books, *Forgive My Grief,* volumes 1-4, about individuals involved in the investigation of the Kennedy assassination, including the circumstances of their deaths. His book, *Forgive my Grief II*, provided the names and details of twenty-four individuals who had died that had knowledge of the Kennedy assassination. Bowers was one of the twenty-four individuals. Jones indicated Bowers had died in an unusual one-car accident, had received death threats and linked this information to a large insurance policy Bowers had recently obtained. Jones also stated a Midlothian doctor had told him, Bowers was in a strange state of shock after the accident.

Richard Lewis, *The Scavengers and Critics of the Warren Report*, interviewed Dr. Roy Bohl in 1967. Dr. Bohl was the attending physician when Bowers arrived at the Waxahachie hospital. Dr. Bohl refuted Penn Jones's allegation Bowers was in a strange state of shock.

The commission determined, based upon the Lewis documentation, there was no merit to any further investigation of the Bowers' accident by the committee. There were, however, many individuals who continued to claim Bowers' death was not an accident.

Excerpt from the Commission Report

Death #4

Name: Lee Bowers, Jr.

<u>Assassination Connection</u>: Lee Bowers, Jr. was an eyewitness to the assassination of President John F. Kennedy. At the time of the murder he was employed by the Union Terminal Company of Dallas as a tower man in the rail yards close to the route taken by the presidential motorcade. When summoned to testify before the Warren Commission, Mr. Bowers stated that some sort of commotion in the vicinity of the "grassy knoll," near the Texas School Book Depository, had attracted his eye. He further stated that two men were standing on the knoll at the time of the assassination.

At a later date, Mr. Bowers elaborated his testimony in an interview conducted by Mark Lane, a chief proponent of the conspiracy theory as part of his documentary film, Rush to Judgment. At that time he said that the commotion he noticed might have been a flash or a puff of smoke, such as would come from the discharge of a firearm. Penn Jones, Jr. maintains that this statement was the likely cause of Bowers' death.

Date of Death: August 9, 1966

Place of Death: Dallas, Texas, after involvement in a motor vehicle accident near Midlothian, Texas, in Ellis County.

Circumstances of Death: The Dallas Morning News printed a routine account of Lee Bowers, Jr.'s death on August 10, 1966. He died from injuries suffered when his car went out of control and struck a bridge abutment on Highway 67, two miles west of Midlothian, Texas. Richard Warren Lewis, in The Scavengers and Critics of the Warren Report states that the injuries sustained included "a crushed chest, two broken legs, one broken arm and multiple head and internal injuries."

Lewis and Penn Jones, Jr. differed in their accounts of Mr. Bowers' death. Jones maintains in volume II of Forgive My Grief that Bowers was killed in an "unusual one car accident," characterizing Bowers as one of the people "who paid with their lives for their pitiful efforts to tell the story" of the conspiracy allegedly responsible for the death of President Kennedy. Jones further states that the Midlothian physician who attended Bowers remarked that the injured man was in some sort of "strange shock."

Lewis interviewed Dr. Bohl, the doctor who rode in an ambulance with Bowers as it took the dying man to Methodist Hospital in Dallas.

Dr. Bohl...later told Jones that Bowers, while in shock was sweating "like a coronary." Says Bohl: "I made mention to Jones that Bowers was sweating a lot. He was wringing wet when he came in and I wondered because of this whether he had a coronary. The man was in a state of severe shock, the kind of shock you could expect from the type of accident he was in. He was dying."

In view of the existing available facts, in particular the Lewis interview of Dr. Bohl which appears to refute Penn Jones allegations, the case of Lee Bowers does not seem a particularly promising route for investigation by the committee.

<u>Jurisdiction</u>: The subject died in Dallas, Texas, as a result of injuries sustained in an accident in Ellis County, Texas.

CHAPTER 5

The Investigation

Over the last forty-seven years numerous individuals have written articles and books with theories, opinions and alleged facts about the Bowers' accident. The federal government conducted an investigation of the death of twenty-one individuals associated with the assassination, which included Lee Bowers. There was even a 1992 film documentary portraying the events of the Bowers' accident.[9] Without an accident report, I had to "step out of the box" of a normal investigation to locate details of the accident. A starting point was to research the existing publications and documents that included information on the Bowers' accident. I had to determine whether any of the information could be viewed as credible and provide pertinent details. Without a baseline of credible details on which I could develop a working hypothesis, it would be almost impossible to attempt any reconstruction of the accident.

It did not take long to identify a pattern in the material dealing with the accident. The conspiracy theory allegations regarding the accident could be reduced to four basic issues: the car accident was unusual, a second vehicle ran Bowers off the road, he was in a strange state of shock and he told ambulance personnel he had been drugged at a coffee shop. The same four allegations were simply being republished with varying themes and details.

I separated the accounts of the accident into two categories: named and unnamed sources. The details provided by unnamed sources immediately became suspect as it would be extremely difficult to substantiate or cross check the information. I did locate two documents with specific details, which were supported by the identification of the source of the information. The first was Richard Lewis: *The Scavengers and Critics of the Warren Report* (1967).[10] The second was David Perry: *Now It Can Be Told-The Lee Bowers Story* (1992).[11] The credibility of the information in these two publications was based on the similarity of interviews 25 years apart. There were two points in the Richard Lewis information, which I subsequently identified as extremely significant: the description of Bowers' injuries and a statement Bowers died three hours and twenty minutes after the accident. This is an interval that is recorded on the death certificate, which in 1967 could not be accessed without specific permission. Death certificates are not available to the public until twenty-five years after the date of the death. In the numerous books and magazine articles I have read, Lewis is the only person that reported the correct interval. It is also interesting to note, I came to the same conclusions regarding the Penn Jones and Richard Lewis documents as was determined by the 1978 Library of Congress investigation detailed in Chapter 4.

Texas Traffic Laws

I had to locate copies of the Texas Motor Vehicle Traffic Laws[12] and Code of Criminal Procedure[13] that would have been applicable for 1966. The laws that exist today would not apply to the investigation of a traffic accident, most specifically a fatality accident, which occurred forty-seven years ago. I had to identify the legal documents applicable to a 1966 accident. My research would also need to include the reporting procedures by the medical and legal personnel involved with a fatality victim. Understanding the legal climate in 1966 was essential for an evaluation of the actions of individuals involved in the Bowers' accident. Researching Texas legal history was far more difficult than I expected. Numerous modifications to Texas traffic law and the Code of Criminal Procedure have been enacted by the Texas State Legislature over the years.

In 1966, three laws governed a traffic accident: the reporting of the accident, the submission of a written report and the notification of a fatality to the Justice of the Peace. I found the 1966 requirements were essentially the same as they are today. The changes to the laws over the years have not changed the basic criteria.

Reporting the Accident

In 1966, a driver was to immediately notify the local police department if an accident occurred within city limits. If the accident happened outside the city limits, the county sheriff or the nearest office of the Texas Highway Patrol was to be notified. The notification was required when the accident resulted in injury or death or more than $100 in property damage. Typically, this was damage to the vehicle. The law also stipulated notification was to be made by the quickest possible method of communication. This would have been significantly more difficult in 1966 as there were no cell phones or 911 service.

Written Report

The driver of a vehicle involved in an accident resulting in injury or death of any person or damage to property in excess of $100, was required to send a written report to the Texas Highway Patrol Department. If a law enforcement officer, who in the regular course of duty, investigated a motor vehicle accident involving injury, death or damage over $100, the officer was required to send a written accident report to the Texas Highway Patrol Department.

The key word in this section of the 1966 Texas Traffic Law was "IF" in connection to a law enforcement investigation. An officer was not automatically required to conduct an investigation. The law only stipulated when the officer did conduct the investigation then a written report had to be submitted. It was the responsibility of the driver to send the written report to the Texas Highway Patrol Department for any accident when a written report was not submitted by a law enforcement agency.

The 2013 requirements for notification and a written report are essentially the same.[14] Texas drivers are still required to notify the local law enforcement agency for any accident involving injury or death. The property damage requirement, however, has changed and is only applicable if the damage prohibits the vehicle from being safely driven from the scene of the accident. Drivers are still required to file a written report for any accident involving injury, death or $1000 in damage. The wording for the investigation by law enforcement changed from "IF" to "MAY." The parameters for when an officer will conduct an investigation varies based on departmental policy. A very typical example is the investigation of an injury vs. a non-injury accident. It is not unusual for an agency to not investigate an accident that only results in property damage, even if the officer is dispatched to the scene. The drivers of the vehicles are advised to file their own report with the state. There is even a state form, which can be provided to the driver for this purpose. The form is known as the "blue form." The nickname originated due to the fact that for years the state printed the form on blue paper.

The one type of traffic accident, however, that will be investigated by a law enforcement agency is a fatality accident. I have twenty-seven years of law enforcement experience and this has been the established procedure for at least twenty-seven years. The investigation of a fatality accident will be the most accurate of any accident investigation. Officers assigned to investigate traffic fatalities typically have advanced training in accident investigation. I can attest to the fact the Advanced Accident Investigation training course is one of the most difficult I have ever undertaken. Another reason for the enhanced accuracy is due to the filing of criminal charges against a driver who is held responsible for the death of another person. It is not unusual for the case to be referred to a Grand Jury for indictment. As a result, the investigation and report will be subjected to several levels of review, which is not always the case in a non-fatality accident. Even in 1966, a fatality accident would have been investigated by a law enforcement officer and a written report submitted to the Texas Highway Patrol Department.

Justice of the Peace

The third 1966 law dealt with the responsibilities of the Justice of the Peace, commonly referred to as a JP. The Code of Criminal Procedure stipulated when a death had to be reported to a JP. It was the responsibility of the JP, of the county where the death occurred, to conduct an inquest, with or without a jury, to determine the cause of the death. The JP also determined when an autopsy would be conducted. The 1966 Texas Traffic Law required the JP to provide a monthly written report to the Texas Highway Patrol Department for any traffic fatality that occurred in his county. The report was to contain the date and location of the fatality and a brief description of how the accident occurred.

Understanding the role of the JP requires explaining a brief bit of Texas history. A JP is an elected position with the title of Judge. The position does not require a legal background: in other words the person does not have to be an attorney. The JP is responsible for a geographic area of a county known as a precinct. The number of precincts is based on the population of the county. Texas has 254 counties and approximately 900 Justices of the Peace.

The responsibilities of the JP dates back to the frontier days and was originally intended for the investigation of homicides. One of the most notable JP's in Texas history was Judge Roy Bean. He was appointed as a Justice of the Peace in Precinct #6, Pecos County on August 2, 1882 and began calling himself the "Law West of the Pecos." His courtroom was in his saloon. According to legend, Judge Bean used one law book, the 1879 edition of the Revised Statutes of Texas. Newer versions were used as kindling. History has portrayed Judge Bean as the "hanging judge."

The Code of Criminal Procedure governs the duties and responsibilities of the JP for the investigation of certain types of deaths. Over the years, the Texas State Legislature has modified the law to include investigations for suicides, accidental deaths, which include traffic fatalities and other types of death. In 1955, the Code of Criminal Procedure was changed to add a medical examiner system based on county population. The responsibilities for the investigation of certain types of deaths were transferred from the JP to the medical examiner. Initially, there were only four counties that qualified. Dallas County was one of the four original counties, but did not establish the new system until the late 1960's. This meant that in 1966 the JP was the ruling authority for a traffic fatality in both Dallas County and Ellis County. Bowers' accident occurred in Ellis County. Death was pronounced in Dallas County. This became significant during my research on the Bowers' death certificate and the subsequent inquest hearing.

Legal Documents

Based on the 1966 Texas Traffic Law and Code of Criminal Procedure, three documents would have been applicable to a fatality accident: the accident report, death certificate and inquest hearing report.

Bowers' accident occurred outside the city limits of Midlothian, TX. This was the jurisdiction of the Ellis County Sheriff's Department and the State Highway Patrol. It is probable the State Highway Patrol would have been responsible for any investigation of the accident. Prior to joining the Dallas Police Department in 1988, I spent several years working as a reserve deputy sheriff for a county sheriff's department. During that time all accidents that occurred in the county and outside any city limits were investigated by the highway patrol. Sheriff's personnel would provide assistance at the accident scene but did not investigate the accident.

Attempting to locate the accident report was a long shot at best. An accident report filed with the Texas Highway Patrol Department would have been destroyed after 10 years. Many legal documents have an established retention period and after that date are destroyed. Several years ago the state lowered the retention period on accident reports from 10 years to five years.

I did locate two references to a law enforcement investigation. The first was the Waxahachie newspaper account of the accident. The details of the accident were based on information released by investigating highway patrolmen. This does identify there was an investigation and who investigated the accident. I would have expected to find the information from the accident report, or an interview of the investigating officer, to be included in someone's publications. This was a death that was being promoted as part of a conspiracy in which a president was killed. Furthermore, the investigating officer is a primary source of information for anyone researching the events of an accident, especially when it involves a fatality or high profile victim. I know this to be true, as over the years, I have had to deal with the news media regarding traffic accidents and fatalities for a variety of reasons. The lack of this type of information was very unusual considering the involvement of Penn Jones Jr. Jones was the editor and owner of the newspaper in Midlothian: the Midlothian Mirror. He was also one of the leading proponents of the conspiracy theories that developed after the assassination of President Kennedy. The Bowers' accident occurred two miles from where Jones lived and worked. This literally happened in his back yard. In the 1960's, local law enforcement officers would have been very well known in a small community. Highway patrol officers lived in their assigned area. Jones would have known all the local law enforcement officers, most especially as he was the editor of the local newspaper. Yet, the information in the Midlothian Mirror newspaper article provides minimal details of the accident. It states:

"Lee E. Bowers Jr. 41, of Dallas, died from injuries received in a one car accident, Tuesday, August 9. Bowers, traveling alone in a late model Pontiac, hit a bridge two miles southwest of Midlothian on highway 67 about 9:30 a.m. He was taken to W.C. Tenery Community Hospital in Waxahachie, by a Pat Martin ambulance, and later transferred to Methodist Hospital in Dallas where he died at 1:30 p.m. He was vice-president of Lockwood Meadows, Inc. in Dallas."[15]

Another fatality accident occurred on Saturday, August 13, 1966, two miles east of Midlothian on Hwy 287.[16] The article printed in the Midlothian Mirror identifies the investigating officer, the information provided by the investigating officer, a description of the injuries sustained by the individuals in the accident, specific details of the movement of the two vehicles during the crash and the damage to the vehicles. Two different accidents with similar features: both resulted in a fatality, one on Tuesday morning, the second on the following Saturday morning and both occurred within two miles of Midlothian. Yet there is a glaring difference in the details of the two reports published in the same newspaper: the Midlothian Mirror. The newspaper was a weekly paper and was published on Thursday. Bowers' accident occurred on Tuesday. There was sufficient time to have obtained similar information regarding Bowers' accident.

There are two recorded documents which were published within months of Bowers' death: David Welsh, *the Legacy of Penn Jr.*, (November, 1966)[17] and Penn Jones Jr., *Forgive my Grief II* (1967).[18]According to Welsh, Jones had discovered a series of

mysterious deaths that were possibly related to the assassination of President Kennedy. The Welsh article provided details
of the background and death of the individuals on Jones's list,
which included Lee Bowers. Jones's book dealt with the same
topic. There is no significant improvement in the reporting of
the accident details for either of these documents. The Welsh
article states Bowers was two miles from Midlothian when his
car veered from the roadway and hit a bridge abutment. Welsh
references a farmer (not identified) who saw the car and said it
was going 50 mph, a slow speed for the road and there were no
skid marks. Jones states in his book: Bowers was killed in an
unusual one-car accident when his car drifted into a concrete
bridge abutment at 9:30 a.m. He references two witness (not
identified) who saw the accident and that Bowers' vehicle was
going about 50 mph.

Jones's research for the publication of a book provided less
details than an article printed in his newspaper dealing with a
similar fatality accident. Jones reports the results of interviews
with a doctor and two witnesses but makes no reference to any
interview with an investigating officer. I found Jones's omission
and apparent lack of any valid journalistic investigation regarding the Bowers' accident to be quite revealing and did become a
consideration in my analysis of his conspiracy theories.

The second reference to a law enforcement officer was in the
David Perry document.[19] Perry interviewed Charles Good, who
worked for the Texas Highway Patrol Department. My research
on Officer Good identified he was a special investigator for the
Dallas area.[20] During the events surrounding the Kennedy assassination he was assigned to the command center for the Kennedy
visit and to the post-command center after the assassination.
Good indicated he was a friend of Bowers and often met him for

coffee. Good stated he visited the accident site the next day, but not in an official capacity.

Fortunately, even though I was unable to locate an accident report, I was able to obtain a copy of the death certificate and the inquest hearing report. The information contained in the two documents provided legal details of the Bowers' accident and his death. With the information from the two documents combined with other details I had already identified in my research, I now had sufficient information to start the reconstruction of the accident.

Accident Site

Locating the accident site was critical. Even forty-seven years later, valuable information could be obtained from an evaluation of the location. As Bowers' vehicle had hit a bridge, the construction of the bridge would provide valuable clues as to the type and severity of damage I would expect to see to the vehicle. I could also develop an initial assessment of the type of injuries that would have resulted from the impact to the bridge. The roadway had to be considered: was it straight or did it curve? How wide was the roadway and were there shoulders? The speed limit in 1966 had to be identified. Did the weather play a part in the accident? All are elements that must be evaluated when investigating an accident involving a vehicle that has run off the road and hit a fixed object.

The death certificate, which is one of two identified legal documents exercising authority over the investigation of the accident, established the location as 2 miles west from Midlothian. The Waxahachie newspaper account of the accident placed the location at 3.5 miles south of Midlothian. This was the only document

I located, which indicated a different distance. The reported distances were already problematic, as I did not know where the measurement started. Was it from the center of town or the city limits? That led to another question: where was the demarcation line for the Midlothian city limits in 1966? The difficulty of locating the accident site was further compounded by the fact Highway 67 had been expanded to four lanes and most of the original highway, including the original bridges, no longer existed.

Records on file with the state highway department identified the 1966 demarcation line for the Midlothian city limits. I was also able to determine two sections of the original highway still did exist. The first section extends south from the intersection of 5th and Main St. in Midlothian to the new entrance ramp at Highway 67 and 287. The second section was located on the east side of Highway 67 and extended southwest from Highway 287 to about ½ mile past Ward Rd. This section of the original highway is now the east service/access road.

The original highway in 1966 was a narrow two-lane road with no shoulders. Any loss of control of a vehicle, causing the vehicle to veer to the right, would immediately result in the vehicle being off the roadway. The speed limit in 1966 was 70 miles per hour. Photo #2 is the original section of Highway 67 which extends south from 5th & Main St. in Midlothian. Photo #3 is the section of the original highway that is now the east service road and extends southwest from Hwy 287. Both pictures depict what the roadway would have looked like in 1966 minus the guardrails and shoulders. The installation of guardrails did not begin until the late 1960's. Shoulders were added as new manufacturing plants were built along Highway 67. This is the road Bowers would have driven as he left Midlothian and was headed southwest on Highway 67.

#2

#3

A television production aired in 1992 regarding the events surrounding the Bowers' accident.[21] The portrayed site was part of the first phase of the new construction for the expansion of the highway, which did not start until years after the Bowers' accident. State highway department records confirmed the state did not start buying land for the expansion of Highway 67 until 1966. I was able to locate the October/1966 deed of sale for the purchase of land located on the west side of Highway 67 by the State of Texas.[22]

Based on measurements from downtown Midlothian and the 1966 city limits, I identified three bridges which qualified as a potential accident site. Two of the bridges had been replaced during the highway expansion. The third bridge is located 2 miles from downtown Midlothian and is just Northeast of Ward Rd on the east service road. The east service road is one of the two remaining sections of the original highway. The state highway department records confirmed the bridge had been part of the original highway. The only change to the bridge was the addition of guard rails in the late 1960's. The construction of this bridge, however, is the same today, as it would have been in 1966.

There was also another avenue, which could help identify the location of the accident site: locating property owned by a witness. Several publications alluded to the existence of one or more witnesses to the accident. The only document I was able to locate, identifying the witness, was the David Perry document. The Perry interviews of Dr. Bohl, Barham Alderdice and Noel Coward all indicated Roy Edwards was a witness to the accident. Dr. Bohl was the attending physician when Bowers arrived at the Waxahachie hospital. Dr. Bohl maintained his practice in Midlothian and Roy Edwards was his patient. According to Dr.

Bohl, Roy Edwards stated he was riding his tractor next to the road and the car simply ran into the abutment. Barham Alderdice was the publisher of the Midlothian newspaper and was told by Edwards the car hit the abutment so hard it was like it had been pulled into the bridge. Noel Coward was the ambulance driver for the Pat Martin Funeral Home in Midlothian and transported Bowers from the accident site to the hospital. He also stated Edwards was a witness to the accident. As he was at the scene of the accident, Coward would certainly have known who witnessed the accident. In addition, Mark Bowers, Lee Bowers' son, stated he drove to the accident site two days after the accident. He saw a farmer mowing the fields next to the bridge. Locating the Edwards' property would help identify the location of the accident site. It would also provide additional confirmation Edwards would have been able to witness the accident.

Property records on file in the Ellis County Clerk's office identified Roy Virgil Edwards owned property south of Midlothian on the southwest side of Highway 67. A 1966 telephone book provided an address for Roy Edwards. The Midlothian post office personnel confirmed the address would have been southwest of Highway 67 and in the vicinity of Ward Rd. Ward Rd is the cross street located just southwest of the bridge I identified as the probable accident site. I was also able to confirm the location of the property from Edwards' son, Stanley Edwards. He stated his parents owned 256 acres located on the southwest side of Highway 67.

I cannot state with absolute certainty, the bridge located northeast of Ward Rd on the east service road, is the actual accident site. I can state, however, it does have an extremely high probability as the right location based on the information contained in the death certificate and the relationship of the Edward's property. The bridge, as it exists today, is the same bridge that was there in 1966. This is extremely important, as the construction of the bridge would provide an evaluation of the potential vehicle damage and injuries that would result from a collision that would have occurred in 1966. The bridge represents a piece of physical evidence that still exists forty-seven years later.

The following photos provide views of the approach to the accident site. Photo #4 is a view of the roadway looking north. Photo #5 is a view of the same roadway looking south. The shoulders and guardrails would not have existed in 1966.

#4

#5

Most road bridges, in 1966, did not cross over other roadways but rather were constructed to cross over creeks or ravines. Concrete abutments were placed at an angle on each end of the bridge. Photos #6 and #7 depict the overall construction and placement of the concrete blocks. The view in both photos is the southbound approach to the bridge. Bowers was traveling south. The concrete abutment on the north end of the bridge is the concrete abutment the Bowers' vehicle would have struck. As there were no guardrails in 1966, the vehicle was able to leave the roadway resulting in a head-on collision.

#6

#7

Photos #8 to #12 provide a close-up of the concrete blocks and placement of the concrete abutments. The bridge construction is all concrete and the abutments are large and very solid concrete blocks sunk deep into the ground.

#8

#9

#10

#11

#12

Vehicle and Injuries

The statements attributed to the witness, Roy Edwards, provided an indication of the severity of the impact to the bridge: Bowers' vehicle just drove into the abutment and the vehicle hit the abutment so hard it was like it had been pulled into the bridge. Lee Bowers' son confirmed information, originally provided to David Perry, regarding the severity of the damage to his father's vehicle. He stated the engine of the car was driven back into the driver's seat of the vehicle.

In the Richard Lewis interview, Dr. Bohl indicated Bowers suffered a crushed chest, multiple head and internal injuries, two broken legs and a broken arm. Lee Bowers' son stated his father had massive head injuries. Noel Coward also confirmed Bowers' had severe head injuries. The significance of these injuries can be illustrated by an explanation of the dynamics involved in an impact between Bowers' vehicle and the concrete bridge abutment.

Newton's Law of Motion states that an object in motion remains in motion at the original speed until acted on by an outside force. In other words, an object will keep moving in the same direction until it is stopped by something. For a vehicle that something can be the brakes, another vehicle or in the case of the Bowers' accident, a concrete bridge abutment. When the vehicle strikes a fixed object, such as a bridge, the vehicle's motion is stopped but in the split seconds just after the initial impact, instead of bouncing off the fixed object, the vehicle continues to plow into the object. The rear wheels will continue to spin and lift off the ground. The bumper and grill collapse and the hood buckles back and up into the windshield. The engine block is forced back toward the passenger compartment. In older vehicles, the passenger compartment would compress around the driver causing the doors to buckle and come apart. I have worked fatality accidents where the compression of the driver and front passenger seat compartment was so severe, the lower half of the occupant's body was not even visible. One fatality accident involved a head-on collision with a front seat passenger who was about eight months pregnant. This was not known until she was extracted from the vehicle as the entire front of the vehicle was compressed around both her and her husband, who was the driver.

Everything inside the vehicle, driver, passengers and objects, are also moving at the same rate of speed as the vehicle. In older vehicles, what would stop the forward motion of the occupants was the impact to the steering wheel, dashboard and other interior structure of the vehicle. Every accident actually has three separate impacts. The first impact occurs when the vehicle hits an object. The second impact occurs when the occupants hit the structure inside the vehicle such as the steering wheel, dashboard, doors and windshield. The third impact involves the organs inside the body which are also moving at the same speed as the vehicle. Movable organs such as the brain, heart, liver and spleen hit the skull, sternum, ribs, spine and pelvis. Chest and internal injuries will result from the impact to the steering wheel and dashboard. Head injuries result from the impact to the steering wheel, windshield, doors and other interior structure of the vehicle. Broken limbs result from the impact to the steering wheel or dashboard.

Bowers was driving a 1965 Pontiac Catalina convertible. Bowers' son did state the top was up on the vehicle. The interior construction of this vehicle would have added to the severity of the injuries. In 1966, the federal government passed the National Traffic & Motor Vehicle Safety Act, which changed the construction of motor vehicles to reduce injuries and death from traffic accidents.[23] A few of the new safety features were impact absorbing steering wheels, door latches that stayed intact in accidents, side view mirrors, shatter resistant windshields, and padding and softening of interior surfaces. Bowers' vehicle pre-dated the new safety features. Photos #13 and #14 are of a 1965 Pontiac Catalina convertible.

#13

#14

Environmental Conditions

The weather conditions on August 9, 1966 did not identify any significant factors which would have affected the accident. The temperature was forecast to be in the middle 90's. Wind was to be from 5-10 miles per hour. Any rain was not expected until the afternoon.

Transport and Treatment

In 1966, the majority of Texas ambulances were owned by funeral homes. The vehicle did double duty as a hearse and an ambulance. Ambulance personal were only required to have theoretical or practical knowledge of first aid as certified by the American Red Cross and the vehicles were equipped with only a first aid kit, splint and oxygen. Enhancements to the Texas Emergency Medical Service did not develop until the late 1960's.[24]

The Pat Martin Funeral Home in Midlothian owned the ambulance that transported Bowers to the hospital in Waxahachie. Noel Coward worked for the Pat Martin Funeral Home and was the ambulance driver that responded to the accident. Noel Coward indicated he believed Bowers was dead when he was removed from the wrecked vehicle, due to the severity of the head injuries. He said he loaded him into the ambulance and headed to the hospital. Noel Coward's statements also provided further insight into the limitations of the emergency services in 1966. He stated there were many occasions when he was alone in responding to an accident. He would be assisted at the accident site by other individuals who were present. This meant, that during the transport, there would have been no one inside the ambulance attending to the victim.

Dr. Bohl met the ambulance at the Waxahachie hospital. Dr. Bohl was interviewed by Richard Lewis and David Perry. The interviews were twenty-five years apart and in both interviews, Dr. Bohl refuted the claim Bowers was in a strange state of shock. He indicated the shock was not unusual considering his injuries. In the Richard Lewis interview, Dr. Bohl provided significant information regarding Bowers' condition in addition to the description of his injures. Dr. Bohl indicated Bowers had been sweating and was excessively wet when he arrived at the hospital. Dr. Bohl also stated he suspected a coronary. The comment regarding the excessive sweating combined with the reference to a heart attack was significant. Considering the severity of Bowers' injuries, his wet condition had to have been excessive to prompt a comment from the attending physician. In 2005, the University of Illinois conducted a study of heart attack symptoms. The study results identified excessive sweating was the number one symptom that would prompt a person having a heart attack to seek medical treatment.[25] It exceeded even chest, arm and shoulder pain. The other significant piece of information provided by Dr. Bohl dealt with the transport of Bowers to Methodist hospital in Dallas. Dr. Bohl rode in the ambulance.

Death Certificate and Inquest Hearing

The death of Bowers was reported to Judge W.E. Richburg, Justice of the Peace, Precinct No. 7, in Dallas County.

Judge Richburg was an extremely interesting individual and was known as the "Law West of the Trinity." He held office from 1944 to 1972 and was extremely popular and well respected. Judge Richburg, however, had a reputation for not always following the letter of the law but rather the spirit of the law. During my early years as a Dallas patrol officer, I heard many stories about Judge Richburg from officers who worked for the department when Judge Richburg was still in office. Judge Richburg was also linked to the investigation of the Kennedy assassination. He ordered the autopsy, conducted the inquest hearing and signed the death certificate for Jack Ruby.

Judge Richburg pronounced the death of Bowers, signed the death certificate and conducted the inquest hearing as required by the 1966 Code of Criminal Procedure. The death certificate includes the following entries.[26]

1) Place of Death, County: Dallas
2) Name of Hospital or Institution: Methodist Hospital of Dallas
3) Date of Death: August 9, 1966
4) Cause of Death: Multiple Head and Internal Injuries
5) Was autopsy performed: left blank
6) Interval between onset and death: instant
7) Time of Injury: 9:30 a.m.
8) Date of Injury: 8-9-66

9) Held Inquest: August 9, 1966

10) Pronounced death: 12:50 p.m.

11) Signed Signature: W.E. Richburg, J.P.

12) Date of Signature: 8-9-66

13) Date death certificate received by local register: Stamped Aug 10, 1966

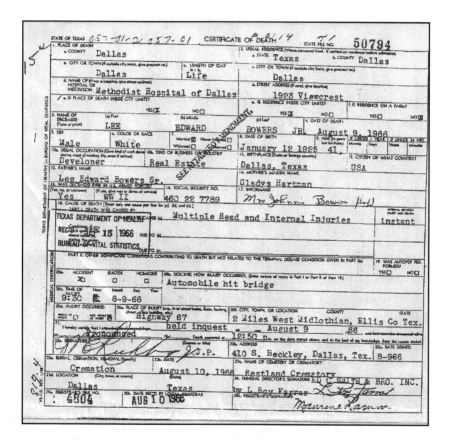

The JP signs the death certificate when a death, stipulated by the Code of Criminal Procedure, was required to be reported to the JP. The format of the death certificate used in 1966 included sections that were not applicable to the JP. A JP is not notified until after the person has died. The JP could not fill in the blanks that would normally be completed by a doctor.

The following are the entries in the Medical Certification section the attending physician would complete.

I hereby certify that I attended the deceased from _____, 19___ to _____19___ and last saw the deceased alive on _____19,___.

Death occurred at _____m on the date stated above, and to the best of my knowledge, from the causes stated.

The JP cannot state he attended the deceased or provide a date when he last saw the deceased alive. The JP cannot provide the time of death as he would not have been present. The Medical Certification section of the death certificate had to be modified. This was a typical procedure in 1966. The following changes were made to the Bowers' death certificate.

1) "I attended the deceased from": was crossed out
2) "held inquest on August 9 66": was typed in the date space
3) "and last saw the deceased alive": was crossed out
4) "Pronounced": was typed in the date space
5) "Death occurred at": was crossed out
6) 12:50 p.m. was entered

Upon notification of a death that requires action by the JP, the Judge was required to view the deceased. This could be at a hospital or at the accident site. The pronounced time of death is based upon the time the Judge viewed the body. It does not coincide with the actual time of death. A significant time difference can exist between the actual time of death and a pronounced time of death. This would be based upon the length of time it takes the JP to arrive at the location of the deceased. It is a common mistake to interpret the pronounced time of death as the actual time of death. This is readily evident in the newspaper articles and publications that referenced a time when Bowers died.

The Bowers' death certificate states the immediate cause of death was "Multiple Head and Internal Injuries." The next column is titled "interval between onset and death" and corresponds to the adjacent entry for the immediate cause of death. An entry would indicate the time interval between the onset of the symptoms or injuries and the actual time of death. The Bowers' death certificate has "instant" entered in this column. This indicates death occurred when the multiple head and internal injuries were sustained, which would have been the entered time of injury: 9:30 a.m. In other words, the death certificate is stating Bowers was killed at the scene of the accident. This will be discussed in further detail in Chapter 6.

I was also able to obtain a copy of the Inquest Hearing document for Bowers.[27] The record of the inquest states:

"I, W.E. Richburg, JP, Precinct No. 7 Dallas County, Texas, after viewing the dead body of Lee Edward Bowers Jr. and hearing the evidence, find that he came to his death as the result of Multiple Head and Internal Injuries-Accidental Death."

Form 199

JUSTICE'S INQUEST DOCKET:

IN THE JUSTICE'S COURT, PRECINCT NO. 7   INQUEST NO. 199

DALLAS COUNTY, TEXAS

IN THE MATTER OF THE INQUISITION UPON THE BODY OF

Lee Edward Bowers Jr.   DECEASED

STATE OF TEXAS   CERTIFICATE OF DEATH   STATE FILE NO.

PLACE OF DEATH — COUNTY	Dallas
STATE	Texas — COUNTY Dallas
CITY OR TOWN	Dallas
LENGTH OF STAY	Life
CITY OR TOWN	Dallas
NAME OF HOSPITAL OR INSTITUTION	Methodist Hospital of Dallas
STREET ADDRESS	1923 Viewcrest
NAME OF DECEASED	Lee Edward Bowers Jr.
DATE OF DEATH	August 9, 1966
SEX	Male	COLOR OR RACE	White
DATE OF BIRTH	January 12, 1925	AGE	41
USUAL OCCUPATION	Developer	KIND OF BUSINESS OR INDUSTRY	Real Estate
BIRTHPLACE	Dallas, Texas	CITIZEN OF WHAT COUNTRY	USA
FATHER'S NAME	Lee Edward Bowers Sr.
MOTHER'S MAIDEN NAME	Gladys Hartman
WAS DECEASED EVER IN U.S. ARMED FORCES	Yes	WW II	SOCIAL SECURITY NO.	460 22 7789	INFORMANT	Mrs. Johnnie Bowers
CAUSE OF DEATH	Multiple Head and Internal Injuries	Instant
DESCRIBE HOW INJURY OCCURRED	Automobile hit bridge
TIME OF INJURY	9:30 A.M. 8 9 66
PLACE OF INJURY	Highway 67
CITY, TOWN OR LOCATION	2 miles West Midlothian, Ellis Co. Texas
Pronounced	8-10-66	12:50 P.	Held Inquest August 9, 1966
DATE SIGNED	8-9-66
SIGNATURE	W. E. Richburg	J. P.	410 South Beckley
BURIAL, CREMATION, REMOVAL	Cremation	DATE	Aug. 10, 1966	NAME OF CEMETERY OR CREMATORY	Restland Crematory
LOCATION	Dallas	Texas	FUNERAL DIRECTOR	Ed C. Smith & Bro. Inc.

FINDINGS BY THE JUSTICE

I, W. E. Richburg .... Justice of the Peace, Precinct No. 7

Dallas .... County, Texas, after viewing the dead body of

Lee Edward Bowers Jr. .... and hearing the evidence,

find that ....he came to his death as the result of

Multiple Head and Internal Injuries - Accidental Death

Witness my hand officially, this the 9th day of August A.D. 19 66

Justice of the Peace, Precinct No. 7

Dallas County, Texas.

I, W. E. Richburg ...., a Justice of the Peace, in and for

Dallas .... County, Texas, do hereby certify that said inquest was held before me, on

the day mentioned, and the proceedings in said inquest, as described above are correct.

Justice of the Peace, Precinct No. 7

Dallas County, Texas.

Article 1012. When an inquest has been held, the Justice before whom the same was held shall certify to the proceedings, and shall enclose in an envelope, the testimony taken, the findings of the justice, the Bail Bond, if any, and all other papers connected with the inquest, and shall seal up such envelope and deliver it, properly indorsed, to the Clerk of the District Court, without delay.

Judge Richburg ruled the death accidental. The inquest document, which included the death certificate, is signed by Judge Richburg and is dated August 9, 1966, which is the day of the accident. Judge Richburg states, as part of the findings, that he viewed the "dead body of Lee Bowers Jr." An interesting side note is the death certificate included with the inquest findings is a typed copy. The original death certificate had several handwritten entries, including the Judge's signature. All the handwritten entries on the inquest copy are typed. Copy machines were probably not a standard piece of office equipment in 1966. An error I found on the original death certificate had been corrected on the typed copy. On the original death certificate the autopsy section was left blank. On the typed copy the box for "no" had been checked. An error was made on the typed copy when August 10, 1966 was added next to "pronounced."

I located one other significant document in my research on the death certificate. Judge Richburg signed an Amendment to Medical Certification of Certificate of Death on August 31, 1966 for the Bowers' death certificate.[28] The amendment contains three sections. Part 1 identified the name of the deceased, date of death and place of death. Part II is the section for the Cause of Death. Part III is the affidavit, which states the following;

"Before me on this day appeared the person who signed the medical certification in Part II above who on oath deposes and says that Part II above is a true and corrected statement of the cause(s) of death of the person named in Part I above.

Signature of Affiant: W.E. Richburg."

The amendment changed the entry for the interval between onset and death from "instant" to "3hrs 20min." The significance of this change will also be discussed further in Chapter 6.

The last area of interest was the section detailing the funeral arrangements. The Bowers death certificate includes the following entries.

1) Burial, Cremation, Removal (specify): Cremation
2) Date: August 10, 1966
3) Name of Cemetery or Crematory: Restland Crematory
4) Location: Dallas
5) State: Texas
6) Funeral Director Signature: Ed C Smith & Bro. Inc. by L Roy Farrer

According to the Code of Criminal Procedure, a JP had to provide a signed document to the owner or operator of the crematory stating either the autopsy was complete or had not been required before the cremation could be conducted. I spoke with a representative of Restland Funeral Home in Dallas. I was attempting to identify whether the death certificate provided the required notification since the funeral home director is required to sign the certificate. My inquiry was prompted by the fact the autopsy section of the original death certificate had been left blank. I was advised a cremation permit is issued by either the Medical Examiner or the JP. The cremation permit provides the authorization not the death certificate. I was unable to confirm whether cremation permits were used in 1966. I also identified that in the 1960's and even up to the 1980's, it was not unusual to have the funeral service the day after the death. I was advised arrangements and procedures were much simpler. It was also not unusual to have the cremation occur after the funeral service had been held, which was the arrangement for the Bowers' cremation.

What is unusual is a cremation in 1966 was rare, especially in Texas. A 2010 study identified the U.S. cremation rate in 1960 was 3.56%. By 2010, the U.S. rate had risen to 40.62%. The 2006 rate for Texas was 23.76%.[29] Even by 2006, the Texas rate was significantly lower than the U.S. rate.

By this point in my research, I had accumulated a substantial amount of information. My results were more productive than I could have possibly envisioned at the start of the project. The process now was to sift through the myriad abundance of details for what would be applicable to the analysis phase of the reconstruction of the events surrounding the Bowers' accident. This is what I refer to as the "connect the dots" process.

CHAPTER 6

The Analysis

The analysis phase of a cold case accident investigation is a process of determining the consistency of the known details of the accident. This includes the assessment of the accident site, vehicle damage, injuries, roadway and environmental conditions, applicable traffic law and any driver/witness information. An example, that is an excellent illustration, is a recent investigation I conducted involving a three car collision on a Texas freeway. Unit #1 struck the back of Unit #2 and Unit #2 struck the back of Unit #3. The investigating officer charged the middle vehicle, Unit #2, with the accident: citing the driver had failed to maintain a single lane of traffic. The diagram and narrative of the accident report indicated Unit #2 was partially in the adjacent lane of traffic at the point of impact. Based on the damage to the front of Unit #1 and the damage to the back of Unit #2, it was physically impossible for Unit #2 to have been in the position on the highway stated by the investigating officer. The officer's conclusion, narrative and diagram were not consistent with the physical damage to the vehicles. The result: the wrong driver had been charged with the accident.

The Bowers' investigation was missing many of the components normally available. As previously discussed, it was necessary to extend the scope of the investigation to include other sources of information that would allow for a reconstruction of the events surrounding the accident. As a result, I was able to identify the construction of the bridge, type of roadway, type of vehicle, vehicle damage, injuries, weather conditions, speed limit, applicable 1966 state law, and other pertinent information regarding the aftermath of the events of the accident.

Accident

The location of the accident site provided valuable information. As soon as I saw the construction of the bridge I knew what type of damage and injuries would result from an impact to the concrete bridge abutment. What is significant, in the construction of the bridge, are the concrete blocks installed at an angle to the end of the bridge. This type of construction changes the dynamics of the collision: the direction of force and the point of impact. The identified severity of the damage to Bowers' vehicle is consistent with a head-on collision to the concrete bridge abutment and supports the statements attributed to Roy Edwards. Edwards' description also provides several additional clues. Edwards stated he was riding his tractor next to the road. This would indicate he would have been fairly close to the accident site and been in a position to see the vehicle hit the bridge. His statements also indicate there was no evasive action taken by Bowers to avoid the impact: either by swerving or braking.

The description of the vehicle damage establishes the position of the vehicle to the concrete bridge abutment upon impact. This is important as it identifies the direction of force as well as the point of impact. This ties back to the concrete blocks located at an angle to each end of the bridge. An engine that is pushed into the driver's seat is front distributed damage which extends across the front of the vehicle. The front of the vehicle, specifically the left front, would have been in full contact with the concrete abutment. Bowers' vehicle would have been off the roadway at the point of impact for this type of damage.

As previously identified, Bowers had a crushed chest, multiple head and internal injuries, two broken legs and a broken arm. These injuries would be consistent with a high-speed head-on collision that resulted in the engine being driven back into the driver compartment. The construction of the 1965 Pontiac Catalina convertible Bowers was driving would have pre-dated the new safety features. The interior design of the vehicle would have increased the severity of injuries. There would have been a significant compression of the driver and front seat passenger compartment. Bowers was probably not wearing his seat belt even though the vehicle would have been equipped with a lap seat belt. In 1966, there was no law in Texas requiring the driver to wear the seat belt while driving and seat belts were not commonly used.

Sequence of Events

During my research, I identified two issues that raised the proverbial red flag. The first dealt with inconsistencies in the sequence of events from the time of the accident to the time Judge

Richburg pronounced death. Inconsistencies which ultimately linked to the irregularities I found in the death certificate.

The time interval for the sequence of events in the Bowers' accident is three hours and twenty minutes. This is the interval between the time of the accident and the pronounced time of death established in the death certificate. I reconstructed a probable scenario of the events which occurred after the accident.

1) Someone who observed the Bowers' accident had to get help. In 1966, there were no cell phones or 911 service. The instructions in the 1966 Midlothian telephone book was to dial '0" for the operator for emergencies. To place that call meant getting to a location that had a landline telephone. This was most likely the witness, Roy Edwards. This was another problem as Edward's transportation was likely the tractor. Whatever the method of transportation, there would have been a delay in even being able to call for help.

2) Another delay would have occurred in the arrival of the ambulance to the scene. The funeral home had to be contacted and given the location of the accident. On a Tuesday morning, they may or may not have been open. There is a possibility the ambulance driver had to be called to the funeral home.

3) Extracting an accident victim from a vehicle is time consuming. An engine that has been driven back into the driver's seat would increase the difficulty of the extraction. It would significantly add to the delay in transporting the victim to the hospital.

4) Once Bowers was removed from the vehicle, he had to be loaded onto a stretcher and placed in the ambulance. Based on the 1966 status of ambulance personnel medical training and vehicle medical equipment, it is highly probable

Bowers received little to no medical treatment before or during transport.

5) In 1966, the trip to the Waxahachie hospital would probably have taken about 15-20 minutes.

6) Upon arrival at the hospital, additional time would have been required to remove Bowers from the ambulance and move him into the emergency room where Dr. Bohl could begin treatment.

7) Once in the emergency room, every possible method and piece of equipment that was available in 1966 would have been used to sustain Bowers' life. This would probably have been IV's, heart and blood pressure monitors, oxygen, etc.

8) At some point, Dr. Bohl decided to transfer Bowers to Methodist hospital in Dallas. Bowers would have to be disconnected from this equipment and moved back into the ambulance with limited medical equipment. Dr. Bohl accompanied Bowers to Methodist hospital.

9) The trip to Methodist hospital would have taken 30-45 minutes and the process of getting him offloaded and into the emergency room had to be repeated.

10) Once the medical personnel at Methodist had determined Bowers was deceased, Judge Richburg's office had to be notified of the death. Judge Richburg would have to travel to the hospital to view the deceased.

11) At 12:50 p.m. Judge Richburg pronounces death.

Once I had reconstructed the chain of events, I realized there were serious disconnects which did not make sense. There was only a short time frame for any significant treatment, which was not logical considering the severity of the injuries. There would have been serious delays in even getting Bowers to the

Waxahachie hospital and even further delays with the transfer to Methodist hospital. Furthermore, Bowers did not die three hours and twenty minutes after the time of the accident. Bowers died at some point in time before the 12:50 p.m., pronounced time of death. This would have further reduced the time available for medical treatment.

This led to the second problem. Bowers had a crushed chest, multiple head and internal injuries, broken legs and a broken arm. Dr. Bohl indicated in one of the interviews that his attention was on attempting to stabilize the patient. Why would you even take a chance on moving a patient with this type of life threatening injuries from one hospital and transport him in an ambulance with limited medical equipment to another hospital that was a 30+ mile trip? Why Methodist hospital and not Parkland hospital? Parkland hospital was the trauma center for the Dallas area. In 1966, Parkland's emergency room was considered one of the most advanced facilities in the country. This was a case of my asking "what's wrong with this picture" as it did not make sense. It was not until I identified the issues in the death certificate that I found the explanation.

Death Certificate

A death certificate is a document of extreme legal significance. Anyone who has had to deal with the estate of a family member can immediately identify with the importance of the death certificate. The death certificate controls insurance settlements, the disposition of an estate and even something as simple as being able to disconnect utilities. The time of death is one of the most critical entries.

The information for the death certificate is provided by multiple sources. A family member typically provides the personal information such as date of birth, parent's names, social security number, address etc.

Information regarding an accident (time, location and description) would have to be provided by an individual who knew the details of the accident. Based on the sequence of events, it is highly likely the same ambulance, driven by Noel Coward, would have been used to transport Bowers to Methodist hospital. Coward would have known the specific details regarding the accident location, time and how the accident occurred. There is also a possibility the law enforcement officer investigating the accident would have gone to Methodist hospital. It is a common procedure for a law enforcement officer to follow up on the status of an accident victim by going to the hospital.

The cause of death, date and time of death and signing of the death certificate would normally be the responsibility of the attending physician. When the death, however, had to be reported to a JP, the doctor could not enter a time of death or sign the death certificate. This was the responsibility of the JP. Even though the attending physician could not complete the death certificate, the doctor still played a very active role in the procedures for finalizing the death certificate. A physician had to provide the cause of death or recommend that an autopsy be performed. The 1966 Code of Criminal Procedure stated the JP would procure the opinion and advice of the County Health officer or a licensed and practicing physician on whether or not to order an autopsy. Neither an autopsy nor blood tests were mandatory in 1966.

The entry in the medical section of the Bowers' death certificate for the immediate cause of death is "Multiple head and internal injuries." "Instant" is entered for the interval between onset and death. Dr. Bohl was at the Waxahachie hospital and had first-hand knowledge of Bowers' condition when he arrived at the hospital. Dr. Bohl accompanied Bowers in the ambulance to Methodist hospital. Dr. Bohl is the logical person to have provided the immediate cause of death, the time interval between onset and death and the recommendation on whether to conduct the autopsy.

Judge Richburg signed a death certificate, based on the medical evidence provided by the doctor, which stated death was "instant." A typed copy of the death certificate was part of the evidence for the inquest hearing. Judge Richburg conducted the inquest hearing and ruled Bowers' death was accidental after hearing the evidence. Judge Richburg signed the Inquest Hearing findings. Judge Richburg signed the affidavit stating the proceedings in the inquest were correct. Judge Richburg signed three documents, which stated the information contained in the death certificate was correct. A death certificate that stated Bowers died instantly from multiple head and internal injuries sustained at 9:30 a.m. from an accident which occurred in Ellis County. A death that could not have occurred in Dallas County as stated in the section of the death certificate titled "Place of Death-County."

Judge Richburg was a JP for Dallas County. Based on the 1966 Code of Criminal Procedure, Judge Richburg did not have the authority to sign a death certificate or conduct an investigation on a death, which occurred in Ellis County. A death in Ellis County, by law, had to be reported to a JP for Ellis County.

On August 31, 1966, Judge Richburg amended the original death certificate and changed "instant" to "3hrs 20 min." What would prompt Judge Richburg to reopen a closed case and amend a death certificate several weeks later? Someone obviously identified the same problem with the death certificate that I found and contacted Judge Richburg. Serious legal complications could have resulted had the death certificate and the inquest hearing been invalidated. Judge Richburg's solution was to change the interval. The change would indicate Bowers died in Dallas County and establish his legal authority to sign the death certificate and the inquest findings document.

What is extremely significant is the fact Judge Richburg entered three hours and twenty minutes for the interval between onset and death. This is an impossibility. The interval between onset and death cannot be the same as the interval between the time of injuries and pronounced death. Judge Richburg would not have been notified until after Bowers had died. Bowers' death would have occurred before 12:50 p.m. and the interval would have been less than three hours and twenty minutes. This amendment does emphasize the inconsistencies and irregularities in the events following the Bowers' accident.

Inconsistencies

Bowers' death at the accident site would explain the inconsistency of a second transport of a critically injured patient in a vehicle whose medical equipment would be questionable. Medical treatment would not be required for a deceased patient.

Bowers' death should have been reported to an Ellis County Justice of the Peace. In this case, the Bowers' accident occurred in the precinct of Judge Harold B. Patton, Justice of the Peace in Midlothian. Judge Patton is also the JP who conducted the inquest hearing and signed the death certificates for the two individuals killed in the second traffic fatality accident, which occurred just a few days after the Bowers' accident. Why was Judge Patton not notified? If Judge Patton was not available then another Judge in Ellis County should have been notified. The 1966 Code of Criminal Procedure stated if the Justice of the Peace for the precinct in which the death occurred could not respond, another Justice of the Peace in the same county was to be notified. In 1966, Ellis County had more than one JP.

In the early 1980's, during my tenure with the county sheriff's department, I worked a fatality accident that occurred late at night. The driver was deceased at the scene. The highway patrol officer investigating the accident was unable to locate a JP, in the county where the death occurred, that would come to the accident site and pronounce death. The hospital would not accept the deceased victim and the victim could not be taken to a funeral home. This developed into a significant problem, as the roadway had to be cleared. The decision was made to move the ambulance with the deceased victim to the sheriff's department facility until a JP arrived. I know this, because as a rookie deputy I was assigned the responsibility of staying with the ambulance until the JP finally arrived. This did not occur for several hours. My point in this example: there was no reason to rush Bowers to Methodist hospital if a local JP was unavailable. The situation could have been maintained at the Waxahachie hospital until an Ellis County JP could arrive. I am certain this would not have been an unusual occurrence for traffic fatalities in Ellis County.

Why was Bowers transported to another county where the JP did not have the authority to investigate or rule on a death that did not occur in his county? Why was he transported to the jurisdiction of Judge Richburg? Did Judge Richburg's reputation play a role in the decision? Whatever the reason, it would have been necessary to maintain the perception Bowers was still alive in order to ensure Judge Richburg had the authority to preside over the investigation. This was not an unusual occurrence for the time period and still existed into my early years in law enforcement. The "golden rule" regarding medical transport was "if in doubt, transport." Even though there were many legitimate transports of deceased victims under the "golden rule" it also provided an opportunity to circumvent the requirement to have the victim pronounced at the scene of the accident. A traffic victim, who was actually deceased at the scene, would be transported under the pretext the victim was still alive when placed in the ambulance and died during the transport to the hospital. This is how they could get a hospital to accept the victim. The practice allowed the law enforcement and ambulance personnel to clear the accident site without having to wait until a JP arrived at the scene. A question still remains as to why Bowers was transported from the accident site to Waxahachie. Was it due to the "golden rule" or was it to circumvent the necessity of a pronouncement at the accident site?

Creating a perception Bowers survived the accident until he reached Dallas would explain several other conflicting details. The first is the speed in transporting Bowers to Methodist hospital. As Judge Richburg could not pronounce death at the Waxahachie hospital, it would have been imperative to transport Bowers as quickly as possible to a hospital in Judge Richburg's precinct. Hence, the transport to Methodist hospital, which was in his precinct. It would also explain why Bowers was not transported to Parkland, which had the latest advancements in trauma equipment and procedures to treat accident victims. It would explain why Dr. Bohl accompanied Bowers. If a doctor at Methodist hospital could not provide an immediate cause of death for the death certificate, there was a possibility an autopsy would have been conducted. I reviewed over a 1000 death certificates that were issued in 1966. Even though it was rare for an autopsy to be conducted on a traffic fatality, the possibility did exist. Dr. Bohl's presence would ensure Methodist hospital would accept Bowers and Dr. Bohl would be able to provide the immediate cause of death, as required for the death certificate. It would explain the inconsistencies in the actions and statements of Dr. Bohl. It would explain why Dallas was entered for the County of Death and "yes" was entered for inside city limits, which was a complete contradiction to the medical evidence.

The problem arose when Dr. Bohl had to provide the medical information for the death certificate and the inquest hearing. Dr. Bohl could not, under penalty of law, have provided any medical information for the death certificate other than what was accurate and true. Dr. Bohl was with Bowers from the time he arrived at the Waxahachie hospital through the transport to Methodist hospital in Dallas. He would have known the exact time of death had Bowers died after arriving at the Waxahachie hospital. Had this been the case, Dr. Bohl would have been able to provide the precise interval for the death certificate. The entry would have been a time interval less than three hours and twenty minutes. It would not have been instant.

The fact does remain, the medical information entered on the death certificate states death was instant. Bowers' death occurred when he sustained the multiple head and internal injuries. This may explain why Judge Richburg amended the certificate and entered three hours and twenty minutes. In my opinion, he was not amending the death certificate to correct an error in the medical evidence. He was amending the death certificate to establish death occurred in Dallas County.

The speed of the funeral arrangements was another identified inconsistency. Bowers' funeral service was held the day after the accident. The funeral notice and the article reporting the accident both appeared in the Dallas newspaper the day after the accident, which was the day of the funeral. Bowers' death was pronounced at 12:50 p.m. The funeral notice had to be submitted to the newspaper by 3:00 p.m. on the day of the accident in order to make the next day's paper. Even though funeral arrangements were much simpler in 1966, this would have been less than two hours to make all the arrangements for a 3:00 p.m. deadline. Mark Bowers stated he was at home when he received the call stating his father had been killed in a car accident. It is highly likely this call came from the Waxahachie hospital. This would provide a more reasonable time frame for setting up funeral arrangements and to be able to provide the details to the newspaper.

Legal Compliance

It is not surprising to find an irregularity of this magnitude regarding the legal proceeding for a traffic fatality. Historically, Texas has had a problem with compliance to the laws that governed the investigation and reporting of traffic fatalities. In 2006, the Texas Transportation Institute (TTI) conducted a study of 900 Justices of the Peace and 13 medical examiner offices in Texas.[30]The TTI study addressed the failure to conduct blood tests and report the test results for all traffic fatalities. The study results identified fifty-three percent of the Justices of the Peace were unfamiliar with the law and twenty-eight percent did not even know the law existed. Sixty-two percent of the medical examiner officers failed to comply with the law. In many cases, the decision to perform the autopsy and conduct the toxicology blood tests was based on the availability of county funds. I was very familiar with this study and had an opportunity to provide input to the project. I had numerous discussions with the project director regarding accident investigations, report errors and the existing problems in obtaining toxicology results to identify impaired drivers in traffic fatality accidents.

In 1966, the lack of compliance or knowledge of the existing laws by the individuals responsible for the procedures involving a traffic fatality was even more egregious. As I stated earlier, I reviewed over a 1000 death certificates issued in 1966. I found numerous errors and questionable death certificates signed by a Justice of the Peace. During my research on the history of the Justice of the Peace system in Texas, I came across an obituary blog that allowed comments to be left regarding the deceased. In this instance, the deceased was a JP from the 1940's through the 1960's. The comment stated the Judge was known for signing blank death certificates and giving them to funeral directors to avoid getting called out in the middle of the night to make a pronouncement. I have no doubt this was a common practice and would have been applicable to many cases throughout Texas during that time period.

Conspiracy Theories

I could not make a final assessment on the reconstruction of the accident and the events surrounding the accident without evaluating the conspiracy claims in relationship to the identified details. Could any of the claims be considered as a viable cause of the accident? I had initially identified four basic claims: Bowers was killed in an unusual one-car accident, he was in a strange state of shock, he told ambulance personnel he had been drugged at a coffee shop and a second vehicle ran his car off the road.

Penn Jones labeled the Bowers' accident as an unusual one-car accident in his 1967 book, *Forgive My Grief II*. The Bowers' accident would be classified as a "run-off-road" (ROR) type of collision. An

ROR accident occurs when a vehicle leaves the roadway and collides with a tree, pole, bridge or other type of object. ROR accidents are considered one of the most deadly of all accidents and account for approximately sixty to sixty-five percent of all traffic accidents and thirty-five to forty percent of traffic fatality accidents.[31]This type of crash usually involves only a single vehicle. Rural roads are more likely to be the scene of an ROR accident. Approximately eighty percent of all accidents that occur on a rural road are classified as ROR. The speed limit is a significant factor as over eighty percent of ROR accidents occur on roadways with a 60 mph or higher speed limit. ROR accidents have been the topic of extensive research in an ongoing effort to reduce the death toll associated with this type of collision. The National Traffic and Motor Vehicle Safety Act was enacted in 1966 in response to the increasing number of motor vehicle accidents and associated fatalities and injuries on the road. In 1966, there were more than 50,000 traffic fatalities and it is considered as one of the most deadly years on record. Furthermore, the Waxahachie newspaper account of the Bowers' accident included a report on the increase in fatality accidents in the county. Bowers' death was number sixteen compared to seven for the same time period in 1965. Bowers' death and three other fatalities occurred within one week in Ellis County.

Labeling the Bowers' accident as an unusual one-car accident is without merit. Bowers was traveling on a narrow two-lane road with a speed limit of 70 mph. Bowers lost control of the vehicle, veered off the roadway and hit a bridge. The profile of the accident is a classic case of an ROR and cannot be considered as unusual when evaluating the type and location of the collision.

The strange state of shock was first reported in November, 1966 in a magazine article by David Welsh, *The Legacy of Penn Jones Jr.*[32] Welsh was reporting Jones's identification of a number of individuals, including Bowers, who had died and were connected to the Kennedy assassination. Welsh stated the doctors saw no evidence Bowers suffered a heart attack. He further indicated a Midlothian doctor rode in the ambulance when Bowers was transported to Methodist Hospital. The doctor allegedly claimed Bowers was in a strange state of shock and it was a different kind of shock than an accident victim experiences. The doctor could not explain it as he had never seen anything like it. Welsh even refers to the doctor as the "old doctor." Penn Jones again references the strange state of shock in his 1967 book, *Forgive My Grief II*, and in the 1967 Richard Lewis interview. I could not locate any credible information to support the allegation Bowers was in a strange state of shock or that the condition was related to the cause of the accident. There is information, however, which does contradict the Welsh and Jones statements. Dr. Bohl not only stated he was the Midlothian doctor who spoke with Jones regarding Bowers' condition, but he was also the doctor in the ambulance with Bowers during the transport to Methodist hospital. In two separate interviews, twenty-five years apart, Dr. Bohl refuted the claim Bowers was in a strange state of shock or that it was abnormal considering his injuries. Dr. Bohl indicated Jones had taken his comments out of context. Dr. Bohl also contradicted the Welsh statement regarding the heart attack. Dr. Bohl told Richard Lewis he suspected a coronary. One other point, Dr. Bohl was 33 years old at the time and certainly did not qualify as "the old doctor."

From an investigator's assessment of the validity of the information provided by Jones, I found it lacking in several areas. As a newspaper owner/editor and author, I would have expected a higher degree of accuracy and detail in his books and magazine articles. The inconsistency in the reporting of details in two separate traffic fatality accidents, less than a week apart, by his newspaper raises a question of his impartiality and motivation in providing factual information. Did he fail to report significant information on the investigation of the Bowers' accident because it would not support his promotion of Bowers' death as part of the Kennedy conspiracy? His reporting of the accident details were certainly inadequate considering the accident occurred two miles from his office. Furthermore, the details have been subjected to unwarranted embellishment with little to no foundation for his claims that Bowers was killed due to his role as an eyewitness to the Kennedy assassination.

The third claim indicating Bowers talked to the ambulance personnel and told them he had been drugged at a coffee shop, is another unsupported allegation. In actuality, the predominance of information indicates Bowers was dead at the scene. The totality of the accident details: the damage to Bowers' vehicle, his injuries, ambulance driver statement, the death certificate and the identified inconsistencies in the events following the accident, would refute the claim Bowers was able to talk to any individual after the accident, let alone state he had been drugged.

The last allegation is the claim Bowers was forced off the road by another vehicle. Once again, I was unable to identify any credible information to support the involvement of another vehicle. None of the statements attributed to the one identified witness, Roy Edwards, included any reference to a second vehicle. Furthermore, the Roy Edwards statements do indicate he observed the accident. The limited details provided by Penn Jones also indicate another vehicle was not involved.

The original source for both the presence of a second vehicle and the claim the vehicle had run Bowers' car off the road appears to have been Officer Charles Good. As an accident investigator, I found a number of problems with his involvement in the Bowers' case. According to a Perry interview, Good indicated he was at the accident site the next day to investigate, but it was not an official investigation. Good allegedly talked to an "old boy" who was repairing fences near the accident site. This individual told Good he saw two vehicles coming down the road, turned away, heard the crash and looked back. One vehicle had hit the bridge and the other had continued down the road. Good indicated he formed his opinion that Bowers had been forced off the road based on the comments of this individual. This individual cannot be considered as a viable witness due to the fact he did not actually see the accident. Good did not even obtain the name of the alleged witness on whose statements he based his opinion.

In 1966, Good was an active law enforcement officer. He was not only employed by the Texas Highway Patrol Department but he was a special investigator for the department. Without a doubt, he would have known criminal law and the procedures for a homicide investigation. In 1966, he should have immediately initiated a homicide investigation if he suspected Bowers' vehicle had been run off the road. Had such an investigation occurred it would certainly have been news in a small community. Jones, in his capacity as the editor of the newspaper, would have been aware of an investigation of this nature. Considering he was attempting to establish Bowers was killed due to his connection to the Kennedy assassination, a homicide investigation would have provided further support for his allegations.

The fact there is no reference or any indication to any type of criminal investigation, as a result of Good's opinion of "foul play," does cast doubt on the validity of his opinion and his alleged investigation. Had he conducted an accident investigation he would have been required, by law, to submit a written report of his investigation. An accident investigation requires considerable time and completion of a number of activities: examination of the accident scene, vehicles, obtaining witness identification and statements, identifying and classifying injuries, diagraming the accident site etc. Furthermore, extenuating circumstance would have to exist, which prohibited the investigation of the accident on the day it occurred, to result in an investigation the next day. In fact, visiting the accident site, the day after the accident occurred, does not constitute an investigation by any law enforcement standards. Good's position as a special investigator was a step up from a patrol officer and as such he would not have been assigned to the investigation of traffic accidents. Additionally, there is there is one newspaper account indicating there was an official investigation by highway patrol officers on the day the accident occurred. Any evidence indicating Bowers had been forced off the road by another vehicle would certainly have been identified, as the responding officers would have had immediate access to the witness. Waiting twenty-five years to initiate the allegation Bowers' car was forced off the road, categorizes his opinion as speculation with no valid support of any factual information. Good provided other information that was also inaccurate. He told Perry the accident occurred on Hwy 287, not Hwy 67, and Bowers was traveling from Mansfield to Dallas. Mansfield is located approximately twelve miles west of Midlothian on Hwy 287. It does raise a question of whether Good was even at the right location of the accident.

During my evaluation of the published documentation on the conspiracy theories, I identified an interesting pattern in the time line versus the origination of the allegations. The first two claims, unusual car accident and strange state of shock, were originated by Penn Jones and first surfaced in documents published a few weeks after Bowers' death. Jones's allegations were addressed in the 1978 congressional investigation which was based on published writings by various authors. The authors involved were identified. There was no mention of any allegation or author in the congressional report regarding the claims Bowers had talked to ambulance personnel and told them he had been drugged or that a second vehicle had forced the Bowers' vehicle off the road.

The allegation Bowers had talked to ambulance personnel and claimed he had been drugged surfaced around the same time period as the claim a second vehicle forced Bowers off the road. In 1992, Robert Groden appeared in a Geraldo Rivera filmed documentary, "Now it Can Be Told, The Curse of JFK."[33] The filmed documentary highlighted Lee Bowers' role as an eyewitness to the Kennedy assassination, his accident and the conspiracy theories regarding his death. In the film, Groden is standing next to a bridge located on Hwy 67 discussing the details of Bowers' accident. There are a number of problems with the film. The section of the highway where Groden is positioned was part of the new construction that did not start until years after the Bowers' accident. The state did not begin to purchase the land for the highway expansion until 1966. Groden indicates a section of the bridge that Bowers' vehicle hit. The construction of the bridge would not have resulted in the identified damage to Bowers' vehicle. Furthermore, Groden states Bowers was run off the road, he held on for another four hours, talked to the ambulance personnel and told them he had been drugged at a coffee shop in Midlothian. This was another case of my asking "what is wrong with this picture?" It certainly demonstrates the progression of disinformation, which has evolved since 1966.

Chapter 7

The Conclusions

The Bowers' cold case accident investigation was an unusual challenge. There were initial hurdles that had to be overcome. Was it even possible to attempt a reconstruction of an accident that occurred in 1966? Would there be sufficient information to form a credible analysis? Could I determine the credibility of the conspiracy theories as a contributing factor to the cause of the accident?

Surprisingly, the most difficult task was not compiling valid information. It was pulling myself back in time to 1966. I could not apply the legal standards and procedures applicable to an accident investigation in today's environment. I had to examine each detail, as it would have been in 1966; the laws, the vehicle, the roadway, the accident site, the speed limit, legal documents, the responsibilities and actions of the individuals involved with the Bowers' accident and even the status of the emergency medical service.

My objective was to conduct an unbiased examination of the documented information regarding Bowers' accident, death and subsequent events. The analysis and conclusions would be based on the relevancy and consistency of the pertinent details utilizing my experience and knowledge of accident investigation, the Texas accident report system and traffic law.

I accomplished, at least to my satisfaction, what I had hoped what would be the end result. I was able to identify a consistent pattern of information to reconstruct the details of the accident and subsequent events. I was able to address the conspiracy theories that surrounded the accident. What I did not expect was to identify another mystery in connection with Lee Bowers' death. A mystery that involved the events that occurred after the accident.

Accident

The reconstruction of the Bowers' accident is based on the consistency of the elements of the identified information: bridge construction, vehicle information, vehicle damage, type of roadway, speed limit, sustained injuries, statements from the witness and medical personnel, and the death certificate and the findings of the inquest hearing.

Bowers' vehicle left the roadway and struck a concrete bridge located on a narrow two-lane road with no shoulders or guardrails. The vehicle struck a solid block of concrete that was an angular extension of the bridge in a head-on collision. The point of impact was front distributed damage, extending across the front of the vehicle, with the heavier damage to the front left of the vehicle. The vehicle's engine was driven back into the driver's seat by the force of the impact compressing the front passenger compartment into and around Bowers' body. The severity of the vehicle damage indicates the impact was at a high rate of speed. There was no identified evasive action taken either by braking or swerving to avoid the accident.

Bowers died at the scene of the accident due to sustained injuries that consisted of a crushed chest, multiple head and internal injuries, two broken legs and a broken arm. Bowers' body impacted the steering wheel, dashboard and interior structure of the vehicle. A number of additional factors would have increased the severity of the sustained injuries. The force of the engine being driven back into the passenger compartment compounded the impact between Bowers' body and the inside structure of the vehicle. It is highly unlikely he was wearing his lap seat belt. A 1965 vehicle pre-dated the new safety standards for vehicles and would have increased the severity of the injuries.

There is a high probability Bowers was either incapacitated or unconscious prior to the impact. This resulted in a loss of control of the vehicle, allowing it to run off the roadway and ultimately strike the bridge. It would account for Bowers failure to take any evasive action, either braking or swerving, to avoid the collision. There are two probable causes of the medical condition. Bowers was reported to have severe allergies. This was previously identified in the Perry document and was also confirmed during my conversation with Bowers' son. The severity of Bowers' allergies would result in intense bouts of sneezing. This could have possibly affected his control of the vehicle. There is a very high probability, however, he suffered a heart attack. Dr. Bohl stated Bowers was wringing wet when he arrived at the Waxahachie hospital and he thought it was a coronary. Excessive sweating is a primary indicator of a heart attack victim. This appears to have been overlooked in the subsequent documents and articles discussing the accident. This may be due to a lack of knowledge or public aware-ness of the significance of the connection between excessive sweating and a heart attack. Considering the severity of Bowers' injuries, Dr. Bohl's reference to Bowers' wet condition does em-phasize its significance. This combined with Dr. Bohl's comment regarding a suspected coronary would support the cause of the accident was a loss of control due to a heart attack.

Based on my experience with fatality accident autopsy re-ports, I do know, it is not unusual for a driver to have either suffered a heart attack just prior to the accident or was already deceased from a heart attack when the injuries to the body were sustained. In 1966, an autopsy was not mandatory and were rarely conducted when the death was due to a traffic fatality. This was unfortunate as the autopsy would have been able to identify if Bowers had suffered a heart attack. Furthermore, the autopsy would have identified whether Bowers died before the impact to the bridge.

Summary

One of the objectives, at the start of the Bowers' cold case accident investigation, was to determine whether any of the con-spiracy theories could have caused Bowers' accident or his death. What I discovered were opinions and theories with little to no factual support. I have no doubt, Bowers' accident was investi-gated by a law enforcement officer resulting in an accident report. The investigation would have identified any witnesses, what they saw, how the accident occurred, the damage to the vehicle, the injuries to the driver, etc. As a newspaper editor, Jones would have known the procedures involved in a traffic fatality investiga-tion and would have had access to the details of the investigation.

This was an unusual opportunity to fully investigate the death of an eyewitness to the Kennedy assassination that occurred within two miles of his office. Yet, this information is conspicuously missing in the reporting of the accident in his newspaper, magazine articles and his second book, which was released just a few months after Bowers' death. The missing details become even more significant in comparison to a second traffic fatality accident reported in his newspaper just a few days after the Bowers' accident. A report which emphasizes the details of a fatality accident investigation based on an interview with the investigating officer. Instead, Jones's information on Bowers' accident and his death is vague and is based on unidentified witnesses. It is not the type of a report that would be expected from a professional journalist and does raise a question as to his motivation. By 1966, Jones was deep into the conspiracy theories regarding the Kennedy assassination. He had started to gain notoriety for his opinions and had already written one book on the subject. The Bowers' accident and death represented another opportunity to further promote his conspiracy theories. Excluding details that did not support his theories would explain the inconsistencies and misrepresentation of information in his publications. Unfortunately, once Jones had published his opinion, it took on a life of its own, despite the fact his statements regarding Bowers' medical condition had been discredited.

Twenty-five years later, another group of individuals added to the conspiracy theories by embellishing Jones's allegations to include: a second vehicle forced Bowers' car off the road and Bowers telling ambulance personnel he had been drugged. Allegations based on unidentified witnesses and the opinion of a law enforcement officer, which lacks credibility due to the timing of his opinion and the absence of any details regarding a formal investigation.

I was unable to identify any credible information which could support the cause of Bowers' accident and death was due to one of the four conspiracy theories. Instead, the pattern and timing of the information indicates a fabrication of information to promote the theory Bowers was killed as a result of being an eyewitness to the Kennedy assassination.

A cold case accident investigation is all about the people involved with the accident: what did they do and what should they have done. There were identified irregularities and inconsistencies in the procedures affecting the death certificate. This does raise new questions regarding the actions of the individuals involved in the events which transpired after the accident. Were the events and actions influenced by the fact Bowers was a high profile victim? Or was it simply a "sign of the time" for the legal environment in Texas history?

Despite the research and conclusions of this investigation, I have no doubt there will still be individuals who will continue to believe Bowers' death was due to what he saw the day President Kennedy was killed. The course of Bowers' life changed, without a doubt, on November 22, 1963. He will be forever linked to the Kennedy assassination and the aftermath of that event. I do not believe, however, the cause of Bowers' accident or his death was connected to or the result of what he saw the day President Kennedy was shot and killed. His death should not be part of that legacy.

By 1966, the research into the assassination of President John F. Kennedy was growing and gaining momentum. Everyone connected to the Kennedy assassination, as well their deaths, were scrutinized. The death of Lee Bowers was no exception. It was another opportunity to add to the conspiracy theories, regardless of whether it could be supported by factual information. This became readily apparent during the evaluation of the research I had accumulated. It started in 1966 and has not stopped, as disinformation of the Bowers' accident and his death is still being perpetuated. There was a *"Rush to Conspiracy"* response to Bowers' death resulting in an unwarranted controversy. The death of Lee Bowers, Jr., while tragic and untimely, should never have developed into a forty-seven year old mystery.

Appendix 1

Affidavit in any Fact

The State of Texas

County of Dallas

Before me, <u>Patsy Collins,</u> a Notary Public in and for said County, State of Texas, on this day personally appeared <u>Lee E. Bowers Jr., w/m/38 of 10508 Maplegrove Lane, Dallas, Texas DA-1-1909</u> who, after being by me duly sworn, on oath deposes and says:

I work at North Tower Union Terminal Co. RI-8-4698, 7 am to 3 pm Monday thru Friday. The tower where I work is West and a little north of the Texas Book Depository Building. I was on duty today and about 11:55 am I saw a dirty 1959 Oldsmobile Station Wagon come down the street toward my building. This street dead ends in the railroad yard. This car had out of state license plates with white background and black numbers, no letters. It also had a Goldwater for "64" sticker in the rear window. This car just drove around slowly and left the area. It was occupied by a middle aged white man partly grey hair. At about

12:15 pm another car in the area with a white man about 25 to 35 years old driving. This car was a 1957 Ford,Black, 2 door with Texas license. This man appeared to have a mike or telephone in the car. Just a few minutes after this car left at 12:20 pm another car pulled in. This car was a 1961 Chevrolet, Impala, 4 door, am not sure that this was a 4 door, color white and dirty up to the windows. This car also had a Goldwater for "64" sticker. This car was driven by a white male about 25 to 35 years old with long blond hair. He stayed in the area longer than the others. This car also had the same type license plates as the 1959 Oldsmobile. He left this area about 12:25 pm. About 8 or 10 minutes after he left I heard at least 3 shots very close together. Just after the shots the area became crowded with people coming from Elm Street and the slope just north of Elm.

Written Signature of Lee E. Bowers Jr.

SUBSCRIBED AND SWORN TO BEFORE ME THIS <u>22</u> DAY OF <u>No-vember</u> A.D. 196<u>3</u>

Written and typed signature of Patsy Collins

Notary Public, Dallas County, Texas

APPENDIX 2

Warren Commission Testimony

Bowers' testimony to the Warren Commission took place at 2 p.m. on April 2, 1964 in the office of the U.S. Attorney located at 301 Post Office Building, Bryan and Ervay Streets, Dallas, Texas. The individual conducting the interview was Joseph Ball, assistant counsel of the President's Commission. Bowers' testimony included numerous details missing in the Dallas statement. This was most evident regarding the individuals he observed in the area of the grassy knoll.

Mr. Ball: Will you stand and be sworn, Mr. Bowers?

Do you solemnly swear that the testimony you are about to give for this commission will be the truth, the whole truth, and nothing but the truth, so help you God?

Mr. Bowers: Yes, sir.

Mr. Ball: Will you state your name, please?

Mr. Bowers: Lee E. Bowers, Jr.

Mr. Ball: and what is your residence address?

Mr. Bowers: 10508 Maplegrove Lane.

Mr. Ball: Dallas, Tex.

Mr. Bowers: Dallas

Mr. Ball: And would you tell me something about yourself, where you were born, raised, and what has been your business, generally, or occupation?

Mr. Bowers: I was born right here in Dallas, and lived here most of my life except when I was in the Navy, at the age of 17 to 21, and I was away 2 years going to Hardin Simmons University, also, attended Southern Methodist University 2 years, majoring in religion. I worked for the railroad 15 years and was a self-employed builder, as well as— on the side. And the first of this year when I went to work as business manager for Dr. Tim Green who operates this hospital and convales-cent home and rent properties.

Mr. Ball: What railroad did you work for?

Mr. Bowers: Worked for the Union Terminal Co. with the 8 participat-ing railroads.

Mr. Ball: And on November 22, 1963, were you working for the Union Terminal Co.?

Mr. Bowers: Yes

Mr. Ball: What kind of work were you doing for them?

Mr. Bowers: I was tower man in the north tower, Union Terminal, operating the switches and signals controlling the movement of trains.

Mr. Ball: Through railroad yards?

Mr. Bowers: Yes.

Mr. Ball: What were your hours of work?

Mr. Bowers: 7 to 3 p.m., Monday through Friday.

Mr. Ball: Now, do you remember what is the height of-above the ground at which you worked in the tower?

Mr. Bowers: It is second story, it is 14 feet, 12 or 14 feet.

Mr. Ball: You worked about 14 feet above the ground?

Mr. Bowers: Yes

Mr. Ball: And the tower was arranged so that you could see out?

Mr. Bowers: Yes; it is windows except for posts that—posts on each corner. It is windows on all four sides.

Mr. Ball: Where is that located with reference to the corner of Elm and Houston?

Mr. Bowers: It is west and north of this corner, and as to distances, I really don't know. It is within 50 yards of the back of the School Depository Building, or less.

Mr. Ball: Did you say that it is built on higher ground, the base of the tower on higher ground than around Houston and Elm?

Mr. Bowers: Approximately the same.

Mr. Ball: Same? It is higher ground than Elm as it recedes down under the triple underpass?

Mr. Bowers: Yes, sir; considerably.

Mr. Ball: And the base of your tower is about the same height as the triple underpass, isn't it?

Mr. Bowers: Approximately.

Mr. Ball: Now, can you tell me why you refer to that as a triple underpass? In our conversation here before you were sworn your description—you described it as a triple underpass.

Mr. Bowers: It is just a local connotation for it since there are three streets that run under it.

Mr. Ball: I see. And how many sets of tracks do you control from your tower?

Mr. Bowers: There are about 11 tracks in the station and 2 freight tracks.

Mr. Ball: that would be 13 tracks that is, the tracks altogether, that pass in front of your tower?

Mr. Bowers: Yes; of course where the tracks converge and cross and split off to various railroad yards--

Mr. Ball: And the tracks are to the north and west of your tower, aren't they?

Mr. Bowers: Well, the tracks are west, but they proceed in all directions, I mean, they are both north and south.

Mr. Ball: Now, you were on duty on November 22, 1963, weren't you?

Mr. Bowers: That's correct.

Mr. Ball: Close to noon, did you make any observation of the area around between your tower and Elm Street?

Mr. Bowers: Yes; because of the fact that the area had been covered by police for some 2 hours. Since approximately 10 o'clock in the morning traffic had been cut off into the area so that anyone moving around could actually be observed. Since I had worked there for a number of years I was familiar with most of the people who came in and out of the area.

Mr. Ball: Did you notice any cars around there?

Mr. Bowers: Yes; there were three cars that came in during the time from around noon until the time of the shooting.

Mr. Ball: Came in where?

Mr. Bowers: They came into the vicinity of the tower, which was at the extension of Elm Street, which runs in front of the School Depository, and which there is no way out. It is not a through street to anywhere.

Mr. Ball: There is parking area behind the School Depository, between that building and your tower?

Mr. Bowers: Two or three railroad tracks and a small amount of parking area for the employees.

Mr. Ball: And the first came along that you noticed about what time of day?

Mr. Bowers: I do not recall the exact time, but I believe this was approximately 12:10, wouldn't be too far off.

Mr. Ball: And the car you noticed, when you noticed the car, where was it?

Mr. Bowers: The car proceeded in front of the School Depository down across 2 or 3 tracks and circled the area in front of the tower, and to the west of the tower, and, as if he was searching for a way out, or was checking the area, and then proceeded back through the only way he could, the same outlet he came into.

Mr. Ball: the place where Elm dead ends?

Mr. Bowers: That's right. Back in front of the School Depository was the only way he could get out. And I lost sight of him, I couldn't watch him.

Mr. Ball: What was the description of the car?

Mr. Bowers: The first car was a 1959 Oldsmobile, blue and white station wagon with out-of-State license.

Mr. Ball: Do you know what State?

Mr. Bowers: No; I do not. I would know it, I could identify it, I think, if I looked at a list.

Mr. Ball: And, it had something else, some bumper stickers?

Mr. Bowers: Had a bumper sticker, one of which was a Goldwater sticker, and the other of which was of some scenic location, I think.

Mr. Ball: And, did you see another car?

Mr. Bowers: Yes, some 15 minutes or so after this, at approximately 12 o'clock, 20 to 12—I guess 12:20 would be close to it, little time differential there—but there was another car which was a 1957 black Ford, with one male in it that seemed to have a mike or telephone or something that gave the appearance of that at least.

Mr. Ball: How could you tell that?

Mr. Bowers: He was holding something up to his mouth with one hand and he was driving with the other, and gave the appearance. He was very close to the tower. I could see him as he proceeded around the area.

Mr. Ball: What kind of license did that have?

Mr. Bowers: Had a Texas license.

Mr. Ball: What did it do as it came into the area, from what street?

Mr. Bowers: Came in from the extension of Elm Street in front of the School Depository.

Mr. Ball: Did you see it leave?

Mr. Bowers: Yes; after 3 or 4 minutes cruising around the area it departed the same way. He did probe a little further into the area than the first car.

Mr. Ball: Did you see another car?

Mr. Bowers: Third car, which entered the area, which was some seven or nine minutes before the shooting, I believe was a 1961 or 1962 Chevrolet, four-door Impala, white, showed signs of being on the road. It was muddy up to the windows, bore a similar out-of-state license to the first car I observed, occupied also by one white male.

Mr. Ball: What did it do?

Mr. Bowers: He spent a little more time in the area. He tried-he circled the area and probed one spot right at the tower in an attempt to get and was forced to back out some considerable distance, and slowly cruised down back towards the front of the School Depository Building.

Mr. Ball: Then did he leave?

Mr. Bowers: The last I saw of him he was pausing just about in—just above the assassination site.

Mr. Ball: Did the car park, or continue on or did you notice?

Mr. Bowers: Whether it continued on at that very moment or whether it pulled up only a short distance, I couldn't tell. I was busy.

Mr. Ball: How long was this before the President's car passed there?

Mr. Bowers: This last car? About 8 minutes.

Mr. Ball: Were you in a position where you could see the corner of Elm and Houston from the tower?

Mr. Bowers: No; I could not see the corner of Elm and Houston. I could see the corner of Main and Houston as they came down and turned on, then I couldn't see it for about half a block, and after they passed the corner of Elm and Houston the car came in sight again.

Mr. Ball: you saw the President's car coming out the Houston Street from Main, did you?

Mr. Bowers: Yes; I saw that.

Mr. Ball: Then you lost sight of it?

Mr. Bowers: Right. For a moment.

Mr. Ball: Then you saw it again where?

Mr. Bowers: It came in sight after it had turned the corner of Elm and Houston.

Mr. Ball: Did you hear anything?

Mr. Bowers: I heard three shots. One, then a slight pause, then two very close together. Also reverberation from the shots.

Mr. Ball: And were you able to form an opinion as to the source of the sound or what direction it came from, I mean?

Mr. Bowers: The sounds came either from up against the School Depository Building or near the mouth of the triple underpass.

Mr. Ball: Were you able to tell which?

Mr. Bowers: No; I could not.

Mr. Ball: Well, now, had you any experience before being in the tower as to sounds coming from those various places?

Mr. Bowers: Yes; I had worked this same tower for some 10 or 12 years, and was there during the time they were renovating the School Depository Building, and had noticed at that time the similarity of sounds occurring in either of those two locations.

Mr. Ball: Can you tell me now whether or not it came, the sounds you heard, the three shots came from the direction of the Depository Building or the triple underpass.

Mr. Bowers: No; I could not.

Mr. Ball: From your experience there, previous experience there in hearing sounds that originated at the Texas School Book Depository Building, did you notice that sometimes those sounds seem to come from the triple underpass? Is that what you told me a moment ago?

Mr. Bowers: There is a similarity of sound, because there is a reverberation which takes place from either location.

Mr. Ball: Had you heard sounds originating near the triple underpass before?

Mr. Bowers: Yes; quite often. Because trucks backfire and various occurrences.

Mr. Ball: And you had heard noises originating from the Texas School Depository when they were building there?

Mr. Bowers: They were renovating. I—did carpenter work as well as sandblasted the outside of the building.

Mr. Ball: Now, were there any people standing on the high side—high ground between your tower and where Elm Street goes down under the underpass toward the mouth of the underpass?

Mr. Bowers: Directly in line, towards the mouth of the underpass, there were two men. One man, middle-aged, or slightly older, fairly heavy-set, in a white shirt, fairly dark trousers. Another younger man, about mid-twenties, in either a plaid shirt or plaid coat or jacket.

Mr. Ball: Were they standing together or standing separately?

Mr. Bowers: They were standing within 10 or 15 feet of each other, and gave no appearance of being together, as far as I knew.

Mr. Ball: In what direction were they facing?

Mr. Bowers: There were facing and looking up towards Main and Houston, and following the caravan as it came down.

Mr. Ball: Did you see anyone standing on the triple underpass?

Mr. Bowers: On the triple underpass, there were two policemen. One facing each direction, both east and west. There was one railroad employee, a signal man there with the Union Terminal Co., and two welders that worked for the Fort Worth Welding firm, and there was also a laborer's assistant furnished by the railroad to these welders.

Mr. Ball: You saw those before the President came by, you saw those people?

Mr. Bowers: Yes; they were there before and after.

Mr. Ball: And were they standing on the triple underpass?

Mr. Bowers: Yes; they were standing on the top of it facing towards Houston Street, all except, of course, the one policeman on the west side.

Mr. Ball: Did you see any other people up on this high ground?

Mr. Bowers: There were one or two people in the area. Not in this same vicinity. One of them was a parking lot attendant that operates a parking lot there. One or two. Each had uniforms similar to those custodians at the courthouse. But they were some distance back, just a slight distance back.

Mr. Ball: When you heard the sound, which way were you looking?

Mr. Bowers: At the moment I heard the sound, I was looking directly towards the area—at the moment of the first shot, as close as my recollections serves, the car was out of sight behind this decorative masonry wall in the area.

Mr. Ball: And when you heard the second and third shot, could you see the car?

Mr. Bowers: No; at the moment of the shots, I could—I do not think that it was in sight, it came in sight immediately following the last shot.

Mr. Ball: Did you see any activity in this high ground above Elm after the shot?

Mr. Bowers: At the time of the shooting there seemed to be some commotion, and immediately following there was a motorcycle policeman who shot nearly all of the way to the top of the incline.

Mr. Ball: On his motorcycle?

Mr. Bowers: Yes.

Mr. Ball: Did he come by way of Elm Street?

Mr. Bowers: He was part of the motorcade and had left it for some reason, which I did not know.

Mr. Ball: He came up—

Mr. Bowers: He came almost to the top and I believe abandoned his motorcycle for a moment and then got on it and proceeded, I don't know.

Mr. Ball: How did he get up?

Mr. Bowers: He just shot up over the curb and up.

Mr. Ball: He didn't come then by way of Elm, which dead ends there?

Mr. Bowers: No; he left the motorcade and came up the incline on the motorcycle.

Mr. Ball: Was his motorcycle directed toward any particular people?

Mr. Bowers: He came up into this area where there are some trees, and where I had described the two men were in the general vicinity of this.

Mr. Ball: Were the two men there at the time?

Mr. Bowers: I—as far as I know, one of them was. The other I could not say. The darker dressed man was too hard to distinguish from the trees. The one in the white shirt, yes; I think he was.

Mr. Ball: When you said there was a commotion, what do you mean by that? What did it look like to you when you were looking at the commotion?

Mr. Bowers: I just am unable to describe rather than it was something out of the ordinary, a sort of milling around, but something occurred in this particular spot which was out of the ordinary, which attracted my eye for some reason, which I could not identify.

Mr. Ball: You couldn't describe it?

Mr. Bowers: Nothing that I could pinpoint as having happened that—

Mr. Ball: Afterwards did a good many people come up there on this high ground at the tower?

Mr. Bowers: A large number of people came, more than one direction. One group converged from the corner of Elm and Houston, and came down the extension of Elm and came into the high ground, and another line—another large group went across the triangular area between Houston and Elm and then across Elm and then up the incline. Some of them all the way up. Many of them did, as well as, of course, between 50 and a hundred policemen within a maximum of 5 minutes.

Mr. Ball: In this area around your tower?

Mr. Bowers: That's right. Sealed off the area, and I held off the trains until they could be examined, and there was some transients taken on at least one train.

Mr. Ball: I believe you have talked this over with me before you deposition was taken, haven't we?

Mr. Bowers: Yes.

Mr. Ball: Is there anything that you told me that I haven't asked you about that you think of?

Mr. Bowers: Nothing that I can recall.

Mr. Ball: You have told me all that you know about this, haven't you?

Mr. Bowers: Yes, I believe that I have related everything which I have told the city police, and also told to the FBI.

Mr. Ball: And everything you told me before we started taking the deposition?

Mr. Bowers: To my knowledge I can remember nothing else.

Mr. Ball: Now, this will be reduced to writing, and you can sign it, look it over and sign it, waive your signature if you wish. What do you wish?

Mr. Bowers: I have no reason to sign it unless you want me to.

Mr. Ball: Would you just as leave waive the signature?

Mr. Bowers: Fine.

Mr. Ball: Then we thank you very much.

APPENDIX 3

Author Credentials

Certification

Master Peace Officer Certification; Texas Commission on Law Enforcement Officer Standards and Education

Basic/Intermediate/Advanced Accident Investigation, Certification/Instructor; Dallas Police Department

Drug Recognition Expert, Certification/Instructor; National Highway Traffic Safety Administration

Horizontal Gaze Nystagmus/Field Sobriety Tests, Certification/Instructor; National Highway Traffic Safety Administration

Law Enforcement Instructor Certification; Texas Commission on Law Enforcement Officer Standards and Education

Awards

Law Enforcement Professional Achievement Award; State of Texas, House of Representatives

Officer of the Year; Texas Women in Law Enforcement

Officer of the Year; International Association of Women in Police

Officer of the Year, Runner-up; Dallas Police Department

Officer of the Month; Dallas Police Department

Multiple Police Commendations, Certificates of Merit and Citizen/Business commendations; Dallas Police Department and the Dallas community

BIBLIOGRAPHY

Automobile Magazine, Automotive Air Conditioning History, July 2010

Bonar Menninger, Mortal Error: The Shot That Killed JFK, St. Martin's Press, New York

City of Dallas, JFK Collection, Bowers Affidavit of Fact, November 22, 1963

City of Dallas Public Library Archives, Judge W.E. Richburg, JP, Precinct 7, Dallas County, 1966

Corsicana Daily Sun, Charles Good Obituary, May 19, 2012

Dallas Morning News, Weather Forecast, August 9, 1966

Dallas Morning News, Executive Dies After Car Wreck, August 10, 1966

Dallas Morning News, Dr. Bohl Obituary, October 4, 2006

Dallas Morning News, Judge W.E. Richburg Obituary, August 24, 1975

David Perry, Now It Can Be Told-The Lee Bowers Story, The Third Decade, Vol. 9, Issue 1, 1992

David Welsh, The Legacy of Penn Jones Jr., Ramparts Magazine, November, 1966

Ellis County District Clerk, John Chamblee Survey, Abstract No. 192

Ellis County District Clerk, Oil, Gas and Mineral Lease, Roy V. Edwards, Vol. 169, 1952

Ellis County District Clerk, Oil, Gas and Mineral Lease, Roy V. Edwards, Vol. 361, 1967

Ellis County District Clerk, Deed of Record, Roy V. Edwards, Vol. 430, 1953

Ellis County District Clerk, Deed of Record, Roy V. Edwards, Vol. 371, 1947

Ellis County District Clerk, Deed of Record, State of Texas, Vol. 408, 1966

En.wikipedia.org/wiki/List_of_countries_by_cremation_rate

En.wikipedia.org/wiki/File:DealeyPlazaAbove.jpg

Family Search, Texas Death Certificates Archives, 1966

Geraldo Rivera, Now It Can Be Told, The Curse of JFK, May 6, 1992

Gerald Posner, Case Closed: Lee Harvey Oswald and the Assassination of JFK, Anchor Publishing, 1992

Gregory Boyd, Texas Survey Maps, Ellis County, RM Wyatt Survey

Gregory Boyd, Texas Survey Maps, Ellis County, J Chamblee Survey

Harrison Edward Livingstone and Robert J. Groden, High Treason, The Assassination of JFK & the Case for Conspiracy, Carroll & Graf Publishers

Henry Hurt, Reasonable Doubt An Investigation into the Assassination of John F. Kennedy

John Simkin, Lee E. Bowers Biography, Spartacus Educational

Karen Kay Esberger, Images of America, Midlothian, Arcadia Publishing, 2008

Karen Kay Esberger, Midlothian Then & Now, Arcadia Publishing, 2010

Lawrence Altman, For Victims of Heart Attack, Sweating is a Sign to Get Help, New York Times, November 15, 2005

Library of Congress, Congressional Research Service, Analysis of Reports and Data Bearing on Circumstances of Death of Twenty-one Individuals Connected with the Assassination of President John F. Kennedy, 1978

Mark Lane, Rush to Judgment, Holt, Rinehart & Winston, 1966

Midlothian Mirror, Accident Injuries Fatal to Dallasite, August 11, 1966

National Highway Traffic Safety Administration, Run off Road Crashes Report, 2011

National Highway Traffic Safety Administration, Laws Requiring Seat Belts, Vol. 1, Number 6, October 1972

National Highway Traffic Safety Administration, Run off Road Crashes, An On-Scene Perspective, July 2011

National Highway Traffic Safety Administration, Run off Road Crashes, Factors Related to Fatal Single Vehicle, November 2009

National Highway Traffic Safety Administration, Run off Road Crashes, Contributing Factors to Run-Off-Road Crashes and Near-Crashes, January 2009

National Highway Traffic Safety Administration, Fatality Analysis Reporting System, Statistical Reports, Historical Data, 1999-2011

Penn Jones, Jr., Disappearing Witnesses, Rebel Magazine, January, 1986

Penn Jones Jr., Forgive My Grief, Midlothian Mirror Publisher, 1966

Penn Jones Jr., Forgive My Grief II, Midlothian Mirror Publisher, 1967

Richard Warren Lewis, The Scavengers and Critics of the Warren Report, Delacorte Press, 1967

Southwestern Bell Telephone Company, Midlothian, Texas telephone book, 1966 State of Texas

State of Texas, Code of Criminal Procedure, Chapter 49, Inquests Upon Dead Bodies, 1966

State of Texas, Vernon's Texas Statutes, Art. 6701d, Uniform Act Regulating Traffic on Highways, Accidents, 1948

State of Texas, Vernon's Texas Statutes, Art. 6701d, Uniform Act Regulating Traffic on Highways, Accidents, 1954 Supplement

State of Texas, Vernon's Texas Statutes, Art. 6701d, Uniform Act Regulating Traffic on Highways, Accidents, 1964 Supplement

State of Texas, Traffic Law, Chapter 500, Accidents and Accident Reports, 2013

Texas Department of State Health Services, 2000 Emergency Medical Services Regulation in Texas

Texas State Historical Association, Texas History of Forensic Medicine, 2011

Texas Transportation Researcher, Texas A&M University, Legislature Clarifies Reporting Requirements for Fatal Crashes, Vol. 43, September 2007

The Old Farmer's Almanac, Weather History for Midlothian Texas, August 9, 1966

U.S. Federal Government, National Traffic & Motor Vehicle Safety Act, 1966

U.S. Federal Government, National Traffic & Motor Vehicle Safety Act, 1970

Warren Commission, Vol. VI, p284-289, Testimony of Lee E. Bowers, April 2, 1964

Waxahachie Daily Light, Dallas Man Dies From Injuries, August 11, 1966

ENDNOTES

[1] Mark Lane, Rush to Judgment, Holt, Rinehart & Winston, 1966

[2] en.wikipedia.org/wiki/File:DealeyPlazaAbove.jpg

[3] City of Dallas, JFK Collection, Bowers Affidavit of Fact, November 22, 1963

[4] Warren Commission, Vol. VI, p. 284-289, Testimony of Lee E. Bowers, April 2, 1964

[5] Mark Lane, Rush to Judgment, Holt, Rinehart & Winston, 1966

[6] Library of Congress, Congressional Research Service, Analysis of Reports and Data Bearing on Circumstances of Death of Twenty-one Individuals Connected with the Assassination of President John F. Kennedy, 1978

[7] Penn Jones, Jr., Forgive My Grief II, Midlothian Mirror Publisher, 1967

[8] Richard Warren Lewis, The Scavengers and Critics of the Warren Report, Delacorte Press, 1967

[9] Geraldo Rivera, Now It Can Be Told, The Curse of JFK, May 6, 1992

[10] Richard Warren Lewis, The Scavengers and Critics of the Warren Report, Delacorte Press, 1967

[11] David Perry, Now It Can Be Told-The Lee Bowers Story, The Third Decade, Vol. 9, Issue 1, 1992

[12] State of Texas, Vernon's State Statutes, Uniform Act Regulating Traffic on Highways, Art. 6701d, 1964

[13] State of Texas, Criminal Code of Procedure, Inquests Upon Dead Bodies, Chapter 49, 1966

[14] State of Texas, Texas Traffic Law, Accidents and Accident Reports, Chapter 500, 2013

[15] Midlothian Mirror, Accident Injuries Fatal to Dallasite, August 11, 1966

[16] Midlothian Mirror, Two Killed and Six Injured in Two-Car Accident Saturday East of Town, August 18, 1966

[17] David Welsh, The Legacy of Penn Jones Jr., Ramparts Magazine, November, 1966

[18] Penn Jones, Jr., Forgive My Grief II, Midlothian Mirror Publisher, 1967

[19] David Perry, Now It Can Be Told-The Lee Bowers Story, The Third Decade, Vol. 9, Issue 1, 1999

[20] Corsicana Daily Sun, Charles Good Obituary, May 19, 2012

[21] Geraldo Rivera, Now It Can Be Told, The Curse of JFK, May 6, 1992

22 Ellis County District Clerk, Deed of Record, State of Texas, Vol. 408, 1966

23 U.S. Federal Government, National Traffic & Motor Vehicle Safety Act, 1966

24 State of Texas, Texas Department of State Health Services, Emergency Medical Services Regulation in Texas, 2000

25 Lawrence Altman, For Victims of Heart Attack, Sweating is a Sign to Get Help, New York Times, November 15, 2005

26 Texas Department of State Health Services, Death Certificates

27 Dallas Public Library Archives, Records of Judge W.E. Richburg, Justice of the Peace, Precinct 7, Dallas County, August 9, 1966

28 Texas Department of State Health Services, Death Certificates

29 en.wikipedia.org/wiki/List_of_countries_by_cremation_rate

30 Texas Transportation Researcher, Legislature Clarifies Reporting Requirements for Fatal Crashes, Vol. 43, September 2007

31 National Highway Traffic Safety Administration, Fatality Analysis Reporting System, Statistical Reports, Historical data, 1999- 2011

32 David Welsh, The Legacy of Penn Jones Jr., Ramparts Magazine, November, 1966

33 Geraldo Rivera, Now It Can Be Told, The Curse of JFK, May 6, 1992